A TIME TO SOW

A Year of Parables

Francis Patrick Sullivan

1817

Harper & Row, Publishers, San Francisco

New York, Grand Rapids, Philadelphia, St. Louis
London, Singapore, Sydney, Tokyo

For Jeremiah
My Storyteller
(1898–1983)

Scripture verses unless otherwise noted were taken from the New American and Jerusalem versions of the Bible.

FIRST EDITION

Library of Congress Cataloging-in-Publication Data

Sullivan, Francis Patrick
    A time to sow.

    1. Story sermons. 2. Catholic Church—Sermons.
3. Sermons, American. I. Title.
BV4307.S7S85   1989   252'.6   88-45673
ISBN 0-06-067768-6

88 89 90 91 92 HC 10 9 8 7 6 5 4 3 2 1

The *Goban Saor* and his son went for a walk one day.

"Son," he said to the boy, "shorten the road."

"I cannot shorten the road, father," he said, "unless I walk more quickly."

"You are not much good for anything, son," said the *Goban Saor*. "We may as well go home."

They went home. On the morning of the following day they went out at about the same hour.

"Son," said the *Goban Saor*, "shorten the road."

"I cannot shorten the road," he said, "unless I walk more quickly."

"You are not much good for anything, son," said the *Goban Saor*. "We might as well go home."

When they arrived at home, the son told to his mother the words his father said to him.

"Indeed, you are son without sense!" said the mother. "When your father tells you to shorten the road tomorrow, begin a story, and I guarantee you that he will not bring you home."

On the morning of the following day they went out again.

"Son," said the *Goban Saor*, "shorten the road."

The son began a story, and they did not go back this time, but they continued to the end of the journey.

translated by
Dr. Francis McGlaughlin

Contents

Preface

The fictions that follow were written as parts of homilies to engage the creativity of the hearer and invite the hearer to share in the making of sense about scripture and life. And that is what has happened. The fictions are mainly secular, but prompted by sacred texts, trigger texts. The one is not subordinated to the other. The result is an intensification of both the sacred and the secular. For they both face the same human problems. So they belong together in a conversation of compassion whose primary goal is to cherish human beings. The Lord said whoever does so is kindred, whoever does not must be sought and found and spoken to. And more than the Lord have said the same.

1. A Cat and a Cataclysm

For the First Sunday of Advent

Portents will appear in sun, moon, and stars. On earth nations will stand helpless, not knowing which way to turn from the roar and surge of the sea; men will faint with terror at the thought of all that is coming upon the world; for the celestial powers will be shaken. And then they will see the Son of Man coming on a cloud with great power and glory.

LUKE 21: 25–27

An earthquake shook a man awake one night. Bang! He felt it through the mattress first. Then heard it. He lay in a strange silence then, in a strange hotel, in a strange land for him, the high valley of Oaxaca, Mexico. The aftershocks came and he thought he was inside a belly dancer. The springs of the metal bed creaked. He heard the sound of falling glass in the atrium outside his gallery room. He was out of the bed and in the doorway like a snap, one hand to the light switch, the other to the doorknob, just as the squeaking, shivering quake passed around some corner and disappeared, and there was silence. And he was himself alone in a lit doorway looking across the atrium at silent, dark rooms.

He was an architect, visiting in Oaxaca to study how old buildings took earthquakes and how new ones did not. He patted the wall of the gallery and said, "Nice going." He looked back into his room and there were cockroaches running up and down and around the walls and ceiling, some falling off onto his bed, some into his shoes, all trying to find a way out. "They may have the only brains in the place," he thought. So he shook them out of his clothes, dressed, and went down the stairs, hoping they had not been weakened, and came to the porter's desk in the lobby. The porter was asleep in a chair. The man rang the bell lightly and the porter opened two eyes the way someone looks up from a delicious dessert.

"You felt no earthquake?" the man asked.

"Not important," the porter said and waited.

"Nothing will croak in this place?" the man asked further.

"No reason to," the porter said. And his eyes began to close down on his dessert.

So the man turned and went back upstairs, kept going beyond his own floor to the roof, the part that must have swayed the most, to see if there were any signs of damage. The roof was like a patio, full of pots of plants and small fountains and scattered parasols with tables underneath, all discernible in the dark. A few of the plants had been shaken off the parapet. Some water shaken out of the bowls was squishy underfoot. Otherwise everything was intact. So the man took a deep breath and looked up and in the blink of an eye saw several shooting stars. And he saw the sliver of a moon standing on its hands on top of one of the mountains. The sky was alive with activity. "Heavenly cockroaches," the man thought.

He sat to watch, and the activity overhead was furious. "Like the end of the world," he thought. He heard a purr then felt a plop in his lap as a cat landed there from the parapet. He was startled a bit but didn't move. "Heavenly cat," he thought. And the cat explored him buzzing with pleasure, stood up on his lap in a slow motion until it could lick his chin with rough but delicate licks. So the man decided to purr himself, which he did, and the cat loved it and licked him lightly some more. Then it sat slowly down on his lap. And the man moved the hand the cat could see very slowly so he could stroke the cat—which he did to its delight. "Rich cat," he thought as he touched a fancy flea collar. "Fat cat, too," he thought as he ran his hand along the angora fur to the bushy tail which was like a branch he pushed down to have it spring back up again. "I have a cat and a cataclysm on the same night," he thought. The cat yawned and tightened and sank some claws in the man's thigh.

"Ooww," said the man very softly and ran his hand under the cat's paws and lifted them free. "You're a tom all right," he said, and he settled the cat in a more comfortable ball of fur and let it drift off to sleep.

"So when the end comes, all of this will be smashed," he thought as he looked up and saw the streaks of the meteorites and the fierce flashing of the stars in the unpolluted sky and the moon now free of the mountain but still standing on its hands. "Those things will arrive here and pulverize us. And the earthquakes won't stop, everything will be flung around like loose cargo. Better to be a cat. Find a lap somewhere and go to sleep. But there will be no laps. Something's wrong with that scenario." Then he thought further, "The Bible couldn't mean it. Maybe Jesus said it to make this world more precious to us. Cataclysms only scare you until you're dead or they're over. Then you get scared for everything else."

The cat woke and rolled over in his lap. And the man purred his pleasure at this great act of confidence. So he tickled the cat very lightly on the chest, and the cat loved it, wrapping his legs around the man's fingers and wriggling with pleasure. There was a bang again, and the cat whipped into a crouch, claws in the man's thigh, and again a silence while the man freed the claws, then the long quivering, creaking aftershock of the second quake, less than the first. A few more plants went down, some more water spilled, then the strange silence of unbroken sleep all around. "They'll never know what hits them," the man thought. "Just cockroaches and cats know. Some choice I have."

Then he looked up at the sky and said, "You'd be crazy to do it." The cat jumped to his shoulder and walked around behind his head so that the tail was brushing his cheek up and down and the head was purring in the ear opposite. "Crazy," the man said.

2. The Make-Believe Christian

For the Second Sunday of Advent

A voice crying aloud in the wilderness,
"Prepare a way for the Lord;
clear a straight path for him
Every ravine shall be filled in,
and every mountain and hill levelled;
the corners shall be straightened,
and the rugged ways made smooth;
and all mankind shall see God's
deliverance."

LUKE 3:4–6

A Buddhist monk found a Christian child abandoned on the road one day. The child was wearing a wooden cross around her neck and a cotton T-shirt that draped around her tiny frame.

"She's only five years old," the monk thought. There were a few Christians in the area, but he did not know where. Then he met a traveling priest whom he stopped, asking him to take the child. The priest said, "I am about to die. I have just the strength to get myself home. She would be abandoned again after a few miles." And the priest stood there for the monk's response.

The monk said, "I am not allowed to deal with women, young or old. I will lose myself."

"Then leave us here," the priest said.

"No," said the monk, "it will be worse for me if I leave her with you. I will take her until I find someone. May you find peace in death."

"And may you find peace in life," the priest responded, and he left that place.

"Take hold of my robe," said the monk to the child, "and we will walk until we find someone for you." But he found no one to care for her, to teach the girl child. People thought he was a monk gone bad, that this was his own child whom he pretended was a Christian. He got less and less food in his begging for the two of them, until her life was in the balance with his own. So he said, "I will become a Christian for the time that she is growing, and I will care for her, and I will teach her, then let her go in her maturity, and she will find her own. I will then return to my own belief, and may I be forgiven."

So he taught her about creation, and she said, "Oh, how good that is!" Then he taught her about destruction, and she said, "Oh how bad!" Then he taught her about the Christ who absorbed destruction in order to recreate the world, and she said, "Oh, how good he is!" Then he taught her about the judgment, and the paradise, and the place of punished souls, and she said, "Oh, how good and bad that is!" Then he taught her about herself, and she said, "Oh, how good and bad I am!"

But he taught her nothing about himself, until the day she asked, the day of her maturity.

"I am as good and bad as you," he said. "I left what I believed because there was no one to teach you what you believed."

"Will you be punished?" she said.

"Yes," he said, "I will return to life in a lower state until I have purged this sin."

"No," she said, "I will change my belief and become like you so all your teaching will have led me to your way."

"Then you will suffer punishment for me, and that I could not bear. And you will lose the precious things I taught you."

"How can you call them precious? You do not believe them."

"I believe them for you," he said. "They have made you into everything I love."

"I do not understand," she said, "you are everything I love and nothing I believe."

"Then we have a truth," he said, "and maybe not a punishment. I shall have to see. I am close to death, as the priest was to whom I tried to give you."

"If he had taken charge of me, we would have both died."

"Yes," the monk said.

"If you had obeyed your rules and never touched me, I would also have died," she said.

"Yes," he said.

"Is that how you came to understand the Christ for me?"

"Yes," he said. "And now I have to leave the Christ to you for my own death."

"Let me go with you as myself. I'm thin enough to look like a boy or girl. I look like you, I talk like you, and in this robe you gave me I can still be everything you taught me."

"It is good!" he said. "You give me back myself. There is nothing more to hold me."

3. Moon Strikes Woman

For the Third Sunday of Advent

The people asked him, "Then what are we to do?" He replied, "The man with two shirts must share with him who has none, and anyone who has food must do the same."

LUKE 3:10-11

There was a woman who loved to think. She had been fooled so often when she was young that, as she got older, she even wondered what her husband and children meant when they said "I love you." Not that she disbelieved. She just thought, "Some days they mean it because they're happy, some days because they need me, and some days they are setting me up for a heavy demand. Or keeping me from knowing what they are doing." But she didn't say anything to them, because she saw her own "I love you" meant many things in many different ways.

She worked in a library afternoons. And as she walked home—she lived in the city—she used to stop in at an Oratory for half an hour, not so much to pray as to think. The oratory was street level and had a portico in front of it with two wonderful marble columns and a small covered courtyard before the two steps leading up to the door, like the entrance to a hotel, but smaller. There was a neutral zone between the profane and the sacred. And that was often the problem. A beggar could accost you in that space, as one did this day when she approached. It was a gypsy woman striding between the columns. She had on red running-tog pants, over them a multi-colored skirt, a green jacket with red patch pockets, and she wore a ski cap that was gold and had a yellow, long tassel ending in a pompon. "I don't need this," the woman on the way from work said to herself. So she crossed the street to look in shop windows and wait, maybe the gypsy woman would go away. "What am I doing?" she thought. So she recrossed the street and went to the portico and started to go in.

And the gypsy woman, who was heavy, moved lightly toward her, cornered her against a column with her belly and with an urgent, passionate voice said, "I need some money for me and my baby."

"Get it from your man," the woman said. "That's where you got the baby."

"You know men," the gypsy said, and began to press her belly into the woman as if to have her share the pregnancy.

"I'm not sure you're pregnant," said the woman. "You could be fat from too much starch."

"Look!" said the gypsy, and she pulled up her skirt and pulled down the jogging pants and there, sure enough, was the round belly of pregnancy and the stretch marks of a few others and the long scar of a Caesarean operation, maybe the last one.

People slowed down on the sidewalk to look, but they only saw buttocks and thighs and wondered what the hell was going on in the porch of a church.

"I can't give you any money," said the woman.

"You're a mother," said the gypsy.

"Yes, but my back is to the wall," said the woman, "and my purse is behind my back."

So the gypsy freed her from her belly, but put two hands on the woman's breasts, ringed fingers, fat fingers, beautiful fingers, beautiful fingernails with solid dirt underneath. Her skirt covered her again but she forgot her pants which descended slowly down her legs. The woman took out five dollars and held it toward the gypsy, who took it with one hand but kept the other on the woman's breast, then made as if to cry like a child for more, saying "This wouldn't buy a beer."

"That's it," said the woman, and she moved against the pressure of the gypsy's hand, backing her away a few feet. Then the woman turned, went into the portico of the oratory and started up the steps.

"Hey, shithead!" she heard the marvelous rich voice of the gypsy say, and she turned. So did the gypsy, her back to the woman. She bent and flipped her skirt up and mooned her big buttocks at the woman who stood in the oratory door. Then the gypsy pulled up her togs and strode with mighty dignity out of sight around the corner from the columns.

"She really has a beautiful ass," thought the woman. "I bet a lot of people think so."

The woman went into the oratory and sat in the back where she could see most of the marble and the frescoes and wonderful flower arrangements on some of the special altars along the side. And she thought, "That five bucks will buy two beers. But not for that woman. She loves somebody. In six months it'll be the baby that does the begging, not the belly. Then bucks for the baby." The woman started to laugh inside. "That gypsy is being taken too. She can't say no. Baby is just drawing everything from her. It'll drink her dry when it's born. But then, that poor little bastard!" Next she thought, "I got a little street drama for five bucks." But then she thought, "What a hold we have on one another!" She saw there were parrot's beak flowers decorating the main altar. "Must have cost a pretty penny."

There was the box in the center aisle marked for flowers, made of oak and three feet high, with a brass slot in it for coins and bills. "It's mooning at me too," the woman thought. "This whole place is mooning at me. Beautiful place. I have to raise my thoughts." So she raised her thoughts to the icon of the mother and child over the altar. It had white roses underneath it. "What can I give you?" the woman asked herself as she looked. "Five bucks won't do for you. White roses won't neither. You're made out of little stones. What if I give you two breasts that still work, a belly that is still fruitful, and a love that hates lies? I am arrogant," the woman thought. "I'll be little bits of bone soon myself. And what would I want?" The broad buttocks of the mooning gypsy flashed across her mind. "Yes," she thought, "that'd be a start."

She got up from the pew, put a dollar in the flower box, still thinking bad thoughts about it, and left the oratory. There in the portico scrunched against a pillar and totally covered in rags, asleep, was someone with a handwritten sign leaning against him or her and a cola carton below it. The sign said, "I am hungry." The woman put some coins in it and said, "And I am not."

4. The Look-Alike

For the Fourth Sunday of Advent

But you, Bethlehem in Ephrathah,
small as you are to be among
   Judah's clans,
out of you shall come forth a
   governor for Israel,
one whose roots are far back in the
   past, in days gone by.

MICAH 5:2–4

There was a man who was a look-alike for a crime boss. He was a librarian. The harshest thing he had ever done was to take *Huckleberry Finn* off the shelf for the local schoolboard, which was on a clean-up-the-world spree. "If you take people's money, you take people's orders," he thought. It hurt him so much to do it that he knew he would have to quit.

So quit he did, and as he walked out the door a huge man came up to him and said, "Got a minute?" Just that.

"Yes, a lot of minutes," the librarian said.

"You're a dead ringer for the boss," the man said. "I'll give you ten thou if you'll sit in a coffee shop with me for half an hour."

"Why?" said the librarian.

"So we'll get whoever takes a shot at you."

"You'll bury me too?" said the librarian.

"Nobody gets hurt," said the man.

"Get somebody else," the librarian said.

"There's nobody else," the man said. And he took the librarian's arm. "And there's no more time, and you're comin'. So no one does a job on your kids or your wife."

The man spoke softly. Not like a thug. Like a lieutenant who made plans too. And he eased the librarian toward a car with a chauffeur in it. "It'll be over in an hour. Just sit with me and talk like we're making a deal."

They got in the car together. The librarian felt no fear, mostly anger.

The man, who was watching him closely, said, "Easy, pal. I meant it about the wife and kids. Now put this on under your jacket."

It was a bullet-proof vest. The librarian put it on, struggling with it in the back seat.

"Got one for my head?" he asked.

"They don't shoot for heads," the man answered. "Head's too easy to miss. Body is what they shoot."

"What about you?" the librarian asked.

The man patted his coat as if to say he had one. In ten minutes they were near the coffee shop, an L-shaped place that was spacious and crowded. "It will be a massacre," the librarian thought. The car drove a block beyond, and they got out to walk back.

The librarian halted and said to the man, "It'll be a massacre in that place. One bullet will hit ten people. I'm not taking another step. I don't care what you do or where you do it."

"We sit where there's nobody," the man said.

"There's nowhere where there's nobody," the librarian answered.

"Last two seats at the bar," the man said. "We're near the coffee machines and the wall and we're looking at one another. You where they can see your face, me where they can see my back. And if you don't there'll be a massacre all right, but in your house, not here. All they want now is you."

"And you've got people there to shoot back?" the librarian asked.

"Not with guns. We don't fight in public. Doesn't help us. Just you and me."

So the librarian and man went into the coffee shop. They waited until the last seats at the end of the bar cleared, talking seemingly intensely as they did. Then they sat and ordered coffee and danish.

After they were served and had a few bites, the man said, "Now turn toward me and start talking like you wanted to explain something to me."

The librarian did. He started talking about Huckleberry Finn and Jim and the house floating down the river with a dead body in one of its rooms. The librarian didn't know what hit him but a blast caught him in his chest and drove him off the seat and against the wall like a sledge, and a second blast hit the man who seemed to be blown right on top of him like a rug. There was pandemonium. He could hear it, so he was still alive. The man on top of him didn't move, so he must be dead. But tables and glass flew all over; feet ran out doors and along sidewalks. He heard the sound of a terrific struggle not far from the two seats, curses and grunts, a snapping bone, and a scream of pain. And then an unbelievable lull against the background of pandemonium.

"Okay, everybody, okay, we're police, calm it, no more shooting, calm it, we've got the guys, it's okay." There were several voices shouting this, and the panic shifted its sound into a kind of whimpering of relief.

"Anybody hurt? wounded? We know you're bruised, but hurt by a weapon? Anybody?"

The librarian felt the bruises on his chest.

"Mick, you okay?" came a voice near him.

The big man moved and said, "No, some got me below the vest." And he slid free of the librarian underneath and sat slowly up. "It's not bad. You got 'em?"

"Yeah," the voice said. "These are the ones. Just like you figured. Can you get up?"

"Yeah," Mick said. "We should look at this guy too. You okay, buddy?"

The librarian sat up against the wall knowing he was bruised, not hurt. His clothes were partly ripped from the shot he took.

"My body's okay," the librarian said.

"That's all that counts," Mick said, and he reached down to pull the librarian to his feet.

"Keep your hands off me," said the librarian. "You do evil to stop evil. You lied me into this!"

"What's he talking about?" said the plainclothesman who was in charge. The place was now furious with another kind of activity, ambulances and cop cars and TV and spectators, more confusion than during the shootout.

"Don't know," said Mick. "Listen, I told you it'd be scary but not deadly. So just let it all out and you'll be okay. We sure appreciate your volunteering for this. No other way we could get these guys."

"You told me you'd kill my wife and kids if I didn't!" the librarian practically screamed.

"You didn't hear right," said Mick. "I said these are the kind of killers who would knock off your wife and kids and not even notice it. But we got 'em and you did it."

He heaved the dumbstruck librarian to his feet and several other police came to put a hand on him then go do some cleaning up and calming down. That's when a TV camera and several mikes nearly did him more damage than the bullet had.

One reporter was already shouting into her own camera, "Look-alike traps Mafia into tipping hand."

Another, "Man poses as Mafia boss. Reveals Mafia killers."

Then the voices turned on him. "What does it feel like . . ."

"Did you this . . ."

"Did you that . . ."

"Please, you people," said the plainclothes chief, "later, at headquarters, we need to check these two out, one's got wounds. Later. Later, all the questions you want."

The police hustled the librarian to a cop car and Mick to an ambulance and both left in a scream of sirens in opposite directions.

"I'm glad you volunteered," the plainclothesman said. "You had to choose fast and you did it. This was our one chance. Found out this morning."

"How did you know about me?" the librarian said.

"People turn you in all the time by mistake. We know you like a friend," the chief said.

The librarian looked at the chief and said, "You know what Huckleberry Finn didn't find out until later about the dead man in the house that was floating down the river?"

"No," said the chief, puzzled. "What?"

"It was his own flesh and blood."

"You just lost me," the chief said.

"You just lost me too," the librarian said.

5. The Bum Who Played Santa

For Christmas Eve Day

Alleluja. Tomorrow the wickedness of the world will be destroyed: the savior of the world will be our king. Alleluja.

There was a bum who went straight once a year. He didn't know how he did it. At Christmas. For 24 hours. He went on the give rather than the take and didn't touch a drop. First thing, this Christmas Eve day, he sat on the library steps downtown and offered everyone a drink from a quart of wine he had stolen from a delivery truck in an alley. He took nothing for himself. He had some pot from a guy who had frozen. He even had some cocaine. He saw where the cops hid it in a dumpster behind the supermarket. He offered this to everyone going in and coming out. He was safe. Cops rarely came near civilized places. But lots of bums came to sleep inside the library and get warm. Few people took his gifts except others like himself who then cursed him for a goddam fool.

A Salvation Army band came along and played some carols on their brass. He waved the jug and the joints of pot at them as if directing, then hoisted himself up and came to them walking sober straight, his beard enough for Santa Claus, and his clothes enough for Kelly the Clown. They let him come into the semi-circle of sound, then closed it around him and launched into a soft carol from Old England. He turned slowly in the circle, his gifts out in both hands, until he ran into the trombone slide, then stopped as if he had hurt something, dropping both the pot and the wine in a smash, splash at his feet. He looked chagrined about the trombone and thought nothing of the mess. But now he had nothing to give. So he began to rock on his feet as they played an old French carol and his face broke into a smile.

He heard another bum shout, "Get the fuck out of there, you'll be eating bibles."

He rocked more, not like a drunk, and he began to feel things, light things, hit him at various places and then go ping on the sidewalk. It was money. People were throwing quarters into the circle. And he began to dance a little more only this time watching his feet, scraping some of the quarters in the direction of the hurt trombone, some toward the trumpet, some toward the bass horn. He shook like a bear and the money that caught in his clothes fell out and he scraped it toward the clarinet. Then he looked up as he circled, hands wide to heaven, more, more, and more came.

The band stopped. He clapped his gloved hands and looked at the mounds of money at each player's feet and saw they were wet with spilled wine and stuck with strands of pot.

"Wait! Wait!" he said, "Wait!" and he stooped and took one pile, scurried over to a bank of snow and washed the money clean. In the process he uncovered some frozen dog poop, threw that into the street, and came back with the snow-encrusted quarters and put them in front of the bass horn.

"Wait! Wait!" he said, and he washed the other piles of quarters the same way and put them in front of each instrument.

"Clean!" he said. "Take it!"

"You take it," said the trombone player. "You need it."

"No!" he said. "No!"

"Gimme that fuckin' stuff," a voice said, and another bum broke into the circle, went down on hands and knees to get the coins.

The first bum simply fell on the second one, who couldn't move, couldn't get at the coins underneath him, and was too drunk to push the one of top of him away.

"Play him a song," he said as he lay back across the man underneath and looked at the sky.

So the Salvation Army played a lovely German carol. The man underneath was using every filthy word he ever knew and his voice mixed with the brass like a cat and dog in a fight. So the man on top simply rolled and put his gloved hand in the cursing man's mouth who promptly bit but the gloves were too thick. There were three pairs.

The music ended and the band broke the circle and moved away, leaving the two men inside a circle of quarters and a circle of crowd which thinned now that the spectacle was over.

"Up, you bastard," the man on top said. And he lifted and hauled the other who, as he rose, tried to grab the quarters.

The first man stood the second on his feet and said, "You get em all, okay?"

"Shit, yes," said the second.

So the first got the quarters and put them in the coat pocket of the second and said, "Okay, come." And he grabbed him by the scarf and pulled him along the street.

"Give that kid a quarter," the first man said.

"Shit, no," said the second.

The first man tightened the scarf. The second took out a quarter. The kid ran for his mother. The mother shouted to a cop. The cop came and rammed the two with his club out of the way. They came to a Santa Claus.

"Give it all to him," the first said.

"Shit, no," said the second.

The first man tightened the scarf. So the second man dropped the quarters like glue off his fingers into the pot.

"You crazy sonofabitch," the second said, and the first tightened the scarf more.

They went back up the street, the first leading the second, people giving them a wide berth. They came to a subway grate with warm air rising from it. They sat down back to back to take full advantage of the heat. They stayed alive that night.

In the morning, the first man said to the second, "Got any money?"

"Shit, no."

"Where'd it go?"

"Down a hole."

"Asshole."

"Santa hole."

"There he is," said the first man.

"Get it back," said the second.

"Hey, give us our dough back."

They got up and went after Santa, who didn't know who the hell these guys were and told them to fuck off.

6. Birth Story: Editor's Choice

For Christmas Mass of Midnight

> And our own people must be taught to engage in honest employment to provide the necessities of life; they must not be unproductive.
>
> TITUS 2:14

There was an editor who needed a birth story by midnight for the morning edition. Christmas morning. He could use the one of the baby born in the rubble of a Turkish earthquake. Mother's shoulders were pinned, her belly somehow unencumbered. There was

another woman, her mother, pinned near her, practically underneath, but her arms were free. She delivered the baby, bit and tied
the cord, before the beams were moved off them both. Happy
ending, with people unable to believe how either mother did it.
No one will be comfortable reading that. Save it for the day after,
maybe.

Then there was the story about the baby born to a woman in
prison. She must have gotten pregnant looking at the moon. People will only read hanky-panky. The baby will disappear. There's
always the one about how younger the mothers get. This one is
eleven. From a hill village in South America. Could be any hill village anywhere. That's a nice bit of bigotry. Maybe the one about
the oldest. Taking a terrific chance. Woman chemistry professor.
Married late. Married one of her students. More for the Guinness
book of records.

Let's see what else. One born in a taxi. Cop delivered it. Mother
and son fine. Need something else, something else. Oh, here is
one that would break you, but everybody knows it. Woman in a
coma, kept alive artificially for three months until baby comes to
term, baby delivered by Caesarean, plug pulled on mother,
mother dies quietly, baby lives, strong and healthy. Wish it hadn't
happened until a minute ago. Great story for Christmas day.

Look at this: sex of baby chosen. Italy. Naples. Before insemina-
tion a girl seed chosen, egg fertilized, implanted, normal pregnancy, birth, first girl in a family where only boys were before.
Vatican loves baby. Hates process. All I need is a fight with readers
on a Christmas story. But what about this? Gimme a blond with
brown eyes. Then a boy with wide shoulders and narrow hips.
The opposite of me. The Cardinal would come in a tank and
demand my surrender.

Here's the one: baby born with good heart, defective lungs.
They keep him alive barely. Other baby born with good lungs,
defective heart. The first one dies. Parents of second one ask for
heart. Parents of first one say yes. Transplant is made. Second
baby lives. Parents of first baby to visit parents of second baby on
Christmas Day. That's it. Background story on doctors who do

transplant. Further story of helicopter crew that braves a snow-storm to get body of first baby to bring it to second. Live baby given the name of the first baby. Got everything. I'll take it.

He sent it off to the press room and sat back and started to tidy the piles of birth stories in front of him with their briefs clipped to each. He saw again the item from Turkey, the birth in the rubble of an earthquake. How did they do it? Mother's pinned from shoulders up, mother's mother is pinned from legs down. He saw there was a story line attached, a series of elements a writer would then have to make into a prose narrative. Grandmother had told her daughter what to do. Had lifted her daughter's legs in the free space. Had counted contractions with daughter. Had told her where baby was, when it began to show. Had told her she had her hands on it, was now pulling it free. Had slapped it. Mother heard cry. Grandmother told her a boy. Had bitten and tied the cord, leaving baby on her chest as she did. Grandmother was covered with fluid and mucus from mother and baby. She was talking to mother and keeping baby crying to clear its passages. Afterbirth landed on grandmother, who kept trying to cover baby with her own clothes and cover daughter with skirts she still had. All this heard by villagers trying to get through spaces in the rubble to lift beams to free both mothers. And seen by two who were close but couldn't lift beams alone.

Wow, people would be stunned. So he started to write it up and realized he didn't know the steps of a birth. So he went to the reference room. It was now close to midnight. And he started to speed-read on the birth process. But that did no good because it was too technical and he needed the old vocabulary people used before science. Names like the names of flowers before they were classified in Latin. But he couldn't find a source.

It dawned on him that this was a world he didn't understand at all, even as a married man with three kids. Two women pinned in rubble bringing a baby into a ruined world. "Maybe I should just connect the sentences in the report. Those who know will get the point." So he did. And he resisted all temptation to make it a symbol of anything, the crazy places anywhere. "Woman's world against man's world. I'll bet a lot of women would have given up. Not these two. They're no symbol. Wonder who they were. Two tough cookies. That mother of the mother. She must have had the instincts of God." He whipped the sheets out of the machine as he wrote and ended up with quite a pile. "Hell, it's good!" he said. So he clipped it. Saw he could still make the midnight deadline. Sent it off to the pressroom, saying, "Find a space." It came flying back in ten minutes. "Can use. But cut to essence. Only 75 words. For free block inside. Ten minutes. Or will use liquor heist." "Use liquor heist," he scribbled on the sheet and sent it off.

He took the writeup of the women and folded it and put it in his coat pocket. "I'll use this for myself. I hope she isn't someone who would kill an Armenian tomorrow or a Christian the day after. Or anyone. How can you scream for blood when you see what blood can really do. Kid covered with it, mother, grandmother. Messy and living. Not messy and dead. There I go, making it a moral. It was just one tough cookie who saved another. And what they saved might grow up to be the toughest cookie of all. Cookie! What am I? Someone left over from the age of jazz?" And he went home.

7. Woman Wanted

For the Mass of Christmas at Dawn

But Mary treasured up all these things and pondered over them. Meanwhile the shepherds returned glorifying and praising God for what they had heard and seen; it had all happened as they had been told.

LUKE 2:19–20

There was a woman whose father was old and in a rest home. He didn't recognize her anymore. The years of disturbance when he felt himself losing ground were over and he was very peaceful. That's what he had been before, a peaceful, generous man. And he had kept her delighted with life until the day she left home for school, then later for marriage. But day was night for him now, and night was day. As the sun rose he went to sleep, and as it went down he woke up. So she had to visit him before dawn or after sunset.

It was Christmas day and she went before dawn. She brought a Bible so she could read the Christmas story to him, as he had done for her and her brother and sister. They now lived too far away to come. He was yawning as she came into the room, as if he could feel the sun below the earth beginning to stir. She put her hand on his head as she had with her babies when they were asleep to see if they had any sudden temperatures. He leaned into her hand as a dog might. "Oh God," she thought, "a dog. A dog is more conscious." So she sat near him as he watched with some inner eye the movement of the sun up toward the horizon.

She opened the text of St. Luke, and began to read: "In those days a decree went out from Caesar Augustus that all the world should be enrolled."

"You will never write your name again," she said to him half aloud. His hand opened toward the water. So she took the glass and straw and he drank some. Then just stopped when he had enough. She saw some color rise in his cheeks, and she knew that was thanks. And it surprised her. So she sat and read on with a small hope that something was getting through.

"And while they were there the time came for her to be delivered."

He coughed a little and tried to put his hand up to close the collar of his bathrobe but couldn't, so she reached over and did it for him.

"And she gave birth to her first son and wrapped him in swaddling clothes and laid him in a manger."

The woman looked at her wrapped-up father. The contrast between him and the Christ child was almost too much to take. She remembered the feeling of the children of her own body as they had made their way down through her and out into the air of life. She finished the line of Scripture: "because there was no place for them in the inn." She remembered when he had taken her first to hear Handel's *Messiah*. He had gotten a balcony seat, front row, so she could stand at the rail and just see over it and watch the great chorus and orchestra fill that hall with sound. So she began to sing the next lines. He had known that whole oratorio by heart.

"And there were shepherds in the field keeping watch over their flocks by night."

She saw the flush appear again on his cheeks as somewhere way inside something was happening.

"And the glory of the Lord shone round them, and they were sore afraid."

"As I am," she thought, "afraid of losing so much and being still alive." He had become very still as if something were missing and he didn't know what. She realized that she had stopped singing and he had sensed it.

So she read a few lines more, then began to sing again, "And suddenly there was with the angel a multitude of the heavenly host praising God and saying . . ."

Then she saw his face now flush full and she guessed that he was hearing the "Glory of God" passage in some inward world. So she stopped and watched, keeping count of the time it took to sing that passage. As the flush quietly left his face she knew it was on the last notes of that chorus. And then she sensed a profound mood of sorrow come over him, a kind of longing. She remembered that mezzo-soprano voice as she had first heard it years ago, "He shall feed his flock." The thought startled her that her father might be hearing that voice right now.

And then his sorrow seemed to deepen, and she thought he must be hearing the soprano next, singing "Come unto him, all you that labor, and he shall grant you rest."

He raised his hand a bit toward the window. She looked quickly to see what he wanted, and saw the light of dawn showing. In fact the snow outside the window was beginning to brighten. So she went and closed the venetian blinds and came back beside him.

He had received the signal that now it was time to sleep. "I'll just finish the story for him," she thought. And she came to the lines, "But Mary kept all these things, pondering them in her heart." "If she was like this she'd have little to ponder," the woman thought. "He's asleep, and he'll never really wake up. He's not here and he's not there.

"Papa," she said, "I love you no matter where you've gone."

She stood again, and she put her hand on his head, the way she had with her own babies. As he surely must have done to her on the nights when she ran a fever.

"The Messiah never went through this, Papa," she said.

His head was warmer under her hand. She'd come in, when she was little, with cold ears, and he would warm them with his hands and pretend to say things, and she'd pull his hands away and say, "What? What?"

"Oh, just something about chocolate cake."

And she'd be in a frenzy to find out what about chocolate cake.

"I'm in a frenzy now," she thought. "To find out what. What happens to my loves. To my father, to my husband, to my children. Something empty like the cold light of morning, Christmas morning, when the story is all over and the shepherds have gone home? No," she thought, "no, there's a mother bigger than I am."

Then a ridiculous thing crossed her mind. For some people mother is only half a word. She looked at him again and she prayed, "Keep him, Holy Mother, my means are not enough for my love."

Then she left. It was nearly full light when she came outside. In that moment, she knew what her father had done. He woke at night to say he was a living death. And he slept during the day to say he was dead to life. "Even without his mind he makes sense," she thought. And she went home with a certain joy in her heart. He had always made sense.

8. A Miss Piggy, a Stuffed Bear

Parable for Christmas Day

> When in former times God spoke to our forefathers, he spoke in fragmentary and varied fashion through the prophets. But in this the final age he has spoken to us in the Son whom he has made heir to the whole universe, and through whom he created all orders of existence.
>
> HEBREWS 1:1–2

A woman was out shopping for Christmas. She and her husband were lawyers. He was in court that morning on a *pro bono* case. A son had knifed and killed his father who had tried to rape the son's fourteen-year-old daughter when the son was out with his wife, and they had come home early and caught him.

She herself took *pro bono* cases, mostly battered wives. She had her baby in a harness on her back, like a backpack. He was at the word-learning stage, so both her ears were wet with pronunciations. And he was heavy. Next time he'd walk. She'd meet her husband at one o'clock, then he could shoulder the burden.

"Sthat?" the boy said, pointing to a model of a Mississippi steamer.

"I'd better not tell you," the woman said, thinking of all the saliva involved.

"N's that?" said the boy.

"A B-52 bomber."

"Bummer," he said.

"Right," she said. And then, "What am I doing here? I'm looking for cashmere turtlenecks."

The boy just gurgled, and she laughed and looked over her shoulder and saw him forming a bubble trying to say "turtlenecks."

She bumped into someone that way, not looking ahead. She felt his buttons and campaign ribbons before she saw his colonel's uniform and impeccable appearance, plus the wings above the ribbons. He had cushioned her with his hands very deftly.

"Oh, I'm sorry," she said. "I have this learner on my back, and he has to see me say things or he mimics me with bubbles."

"Good stage, my wife tells me," said the colonel. There was a quick jump of feeling into his voice and face, but he seemed comfortable with the surprise. "I didn't know mine at this age. I was flying in 'Nam." His voice cooled as he said "'Nam," thinking she might be antiwar.

"One of those?" the woman said, and she pointed to the model of the B-52.

"Yes," said the colonel.

"Bummer," said the little boy.

The woman blushed. "I said the right word to him," she said. "But I do think they are bummers."

"They're cool horror," he said. "I don't fly them anymore. I plan their flights."

The woman heard her son trying to say *horror*, and it came out "aura."

"I'd better let you teach him," the colonel said and made to move around the woman and the boy.

"You could teach me something," she said. "I don't understand cool horror. I'm a lawyer for battered women, but I've got two loves and they're both men. Men fly the cool horrors. Sit with us for coffee if you have time. My husband's not due until one."

"What could I teach you?" the colonel said, still standing there.

"Why?" she said.

"Okay, a coffee shop?" he said.

"Offee," said the boy, "fee, fee," he sneezed. His hood had fallen back. She couldn't reach it so the colonel tugged it up.

"Let's sit here at the bar," he said. "You won't have to get out of your parachute."

They ordered coffees. It was an open place with high stools. The music from the mall was pervasive.

"Sthat?" said the little boy.

"It's a colonel," said his mother.

"Kerna," said the boy, "kerna."

"He flies bummers," said the mother.

"No, I just fly paper now," he said. "I was buying some toys."

"Your children are grown?" the woman asked.

"Are they!" said the colonel. "I have grandchildren. Toys are for them. That's really your question, isn't it? Why am I making life or making love and still working with those bummers?"

The boy buzzed and shot out his arm like a plane and knocked her glasses askew. But she caught them and slid them in a chest pocket.

"It's every question," she said. "What's the soul of this cool horror? The stuff I deal with is always hot and furious."

"Buzz, kerna, bummer," said the boy, "aura, fee, fee."

The colonel was looking at the boy. "I am sorry I missed that stage," he said. "The enemy is not afraid to die. But is afraid to live without power. To be without power is to be in hell. So we threaten that power. To take it away. That means reduce a whole nation to ashes. So their power is nothing and they are alive to know it. It's a calculation we make. It's cool. And it's horror. Whether it's one bomb or a million."

"What about the people?" she said.

"The leaders are nothing without them," he said. "And they are nothing without leaders."

The boy's head sank forward on her shoulder. It was nap time. So she turned a bit and adjusted his head so he could breathe easier.

"I'm thinking on a certain level," the colonel said. "Below that level the argument disappears and the horror heats up. Until we get down to your wife beaters."

"I feel devastated," she said. "Isn't there anyone on that high level that wants to live for something else than power?"

"No," he said. "And it's a good thing they don't."

"Why good?" she said.

"Because they can always be threatened by the loss of it. Something unbearable. Can't threaten them with the loss of love. Or family. Or honor."

"And you?" she asked. "Is it only power for you?"

He was silent and sipped his coffee firmly. He looked at her face without intruding on it. Then looked at the boy papoose. Then looked out at people moving along the mall.

"Can you take it if I tell you?" he said looking back at her.

"I don't think so," she said. "I keep thinking Faust and a pact with the devil."

"No," he said, "not with the devil. Not with an angel either. If this system turned evil . . ." He went so dead still as he said it, his eyes on the styrofoam cup, that she felt a coldness pervade her unlike any other she had ever felt.

"What system?" she said.

"The one you and I live in, this," he said and his hand moved in a slow half circle.

Then she felt herself change from cold to warm, unlike any warmth she had ever felt. "The Russian colonels say the same," she said.

"I know that," he said. "We have to keep the orders from being given. So you see it's a pact with power. The first one who shoots is the demon and is in hell."

She was cold again. She saw him as he presented himself, neither good nor evil, hoping to be good, fearing to be evil, all dependent on who shot first.

"Have I been clear?" he asked.

"Yes," she said. "And you can't trick anyone into shooting first."

"No," he said, "this is metaphysical, it happens to the soul."

"I am in mortal fear," she said.

"I am too," he said, "and it has made me good at what I do."

He put down his cup. Looked at her with the silence of before. Then got up, touched the boy on his hood and left the coffee shop.

The boy sneezed in his sleep and began to struggle awake. "He'll eat me alive and I've nothing," she said.

"Want some cocoa?" she said to him.

He blurred back, "'Oko," as a question.

"Yes, cocoa and cake," she said.

"'Ake?" he said, "'oko 'ake?" He was awake and interested in words again and not fussing. He fell asleep during the cool horror, she thought. She could see the colonel at the toy shop. "Must be for girls," she judged. He had a Miss Piggy and a stuffed bear. "Horror doesn't work on that level."

9. Men into Mockingbirds

For Holy Family Sunday

And be filled with gratitude. Let the message of Christ dwell among you in all its richness. Instruct and admonish each other with the utmost wisdom. Sing thankfully in your hearts to God, with psalms and hymns and spiritual songs.

COLOSSIANS 3:16

There was a man who lost his only son in a war. He himself had survived two wars. He knew what combat was, what being wounded was, what returning to action was. But the death of his son embittered him. He had fought his wars so his son would never have to. Now he was alone, without his wife. She had left him to marry a poet. And without his son. He had been killed in a fire fight in a jungle. His remains were flown home. He was buried beside his grandparents. "Neat, isn't it?" the man thought. "There's no life ahead of me, there's no life behind. You lose your own life, it's one thing. You lose somebody else's and it's hell."

He was sitting on a bench in a city park one day. He never sat on a bench in a park. He usually kept moving, at work as a trucking boss, at home with the house, the garden, the car. But he had shopped this day. He saw a park with some nice trees, an oval pool, and a single-spout fountain. So he pulled up and got out, went to a bench, sat and watched the patterns the falling water made and the ruffles made by the wind.

Then he heard a little voice say, "Get me my ball?" And there was this little kid, his pudgy fingers pointing toward the pool where his ball floated just out of reach.

The man looked around quickly to see who the kid was with, and he saw another guy, like himself, a bit older, looking up into a tree a few yards away. There was a mockingbird in it singing like crazy, and the other guy was lost listening to it.

"Sure," said the first guy.

He looked behind the bench, saw a broken branch, picked it up, and said to the kid, "Show me."

The kid skipped ahead of him to the rim of the fountain pool and pointed to the ball and said, "It's the round thing."

"Right," said the man, went down on one knee and teased the ball back with the tip of the branch.

"Like the monkey with the bananas outside his cage," he thought.

"Here," he said after he rubbed it dry on his jacket. He checked the water quickly to see how deep it was if the kid fell in. Shallow. It would just scare him.

He felt the presence of the other guy near him, heard him say, "Thanks. I'm not the best babysitter."

"It's nothin'," said the first man. "In fact it's great to have a kid trust you. Kids are trained the opposite these days. Have to be. But they sure wake up your love."

"They do," said the other guy. "Not much else does."

"You like that mockingbird?" the first guy said.

"Sure do," said the second.

"It was fussin' and spittin' for a fight, but it sure sounded like a song. Those things can go on for hours." He looked around for the little kid, who was kicking the ball at some squirrels who made panic dashes for the trees. "This way, Matt," he called.

The first guy felt a jolt. His dead son was Matthew. The boy kicked the ball back to them, then began to use the bench nearby as a gymnast would.

"I lost a Matthew," the first said. "In the war. I'm as empty as a used tin can since."

"That war shouldn't have been," said the second. He sounded like a vet as he said it, so it didn't anger the first.

They both watched the boy hanging upside down from the bench, his feet under the back rest; his body on the seat, his head and hair over the edge. He was looking at them, the pool, the jet of water, and giggling, they looked so funny.

"Maybe no wars should be," the first guy said. "I never said that before now. If the reason you fight them for gets killed in the next one."

"Wife gone?"

"Yeah. Married a mockingbird."

The second guy laughed. "They fly away too. You want to work for peace?"

The first looked at the second with some suspicion.

"Yeah," the second said, "I'm a vet. Came home too shot up to work. So if you can't work, you teach, right?"

"Right," said the first.

The kid was now hanging like a sloth from the seat of the bench, his back just above the ground, hanging as if by a thread and he knew it and loved it. Thump! He let go and rolled over on his belly looking for something next.

"You take what you know about war and you tell it to people," the second guy said. "It's not movies anymore. Or the best years of our lives. It's not what made us men anymore either. We're too old to think that now. What we love makes us men, not what we blew away."

The second guy seemed to choke on these words. "My outfit used to be called the best killers around. I never married because there wasn't enough violence to it." He stopped for a minute.

The first guy said, "Who's Matthew belong to?"

"Me," the second said. And he waited. "You don't believe it?"

"Well, yeah," said the first. "I just had to think. It's not automatic."

"I'm in my sixties," said the second. "She's in her forties. She said 'What about it?' She's the biggest risk I ever took. And look at this."

"Boy, that's working for peace."

"You know what could happen to this Matthew too?" And there was a silence between them.

The boy was beside them now, the ball was back in the water, he had the broken branch like a monkey and was teasing the ball along. The two men followed him slowly.

"I can't just work on hatred of war," the first guy said.

"You have the love," the second said. "You lost him, but you still have it. It's when you still love the war you lose. Everything."

Young Matthew lost the ball to the middle of the water. It went in under the spray which made a light drumming sound on it and bobbed it up and down in crazy patterns and spun it one way then another. The boy watched with absolute fascination. The two men watched the boy as if nothing else existed.

10. Should Auld Acquaintance . . .

For New Year's Day

The Lord Bless you and watch over you;
The Lord make his face shine upon you
   and be gracious to you;
the Lord look kindly on you and give you peace.

NUMBERS 6:24–26

There was a man who was going to spend New Year's Eve alone. He was a social worker and Christmas had been a sea of tragedy. He loved the work, but he was pooped. He had a room in an old townhouse. "I'll watch some TV, play some music, go the cold cuts, beer, and bread route," he thought. "Watch the idiocy in New York, then a late movie." The streets in his neighborhood would be jammed, he knew, people going to concerts, to the waterfront for fireworks, to special shows. No night for a tired man to be out.

It was around nine when he first heard his door being tugged at. Not as if someone were trying to open it, but as if someone were trying to pull it through into the corridor just at the head of the stairs. There was a deep bass dog bark too. So he opened the door against the pressure and there on a leash tied to his knob was a basset hound, a young and strong one, booming out barks like a fog horn.

"Hey, hey," said the man as he reached cautiously for the dog and the note tied to the dog's collar. "Please take care of me," it said.

"Just what I need," said the man. He could almost smell the cold air from the person who had just left the dog and slipped out into the crowds in the street. He calmed the dog with the incredibly mournful eyes and too-long ears. Then he brought the dog inside, tied the leash to a radiator, picked up the phone and called Animal Rescue. No answer. Recorded message saying to call in the morning.

"Damn!" he said, "what will Rescue be like in the morning? Okay, dog, I'm stuck. You want some water?"

The dog started to bark its deep booming bark. And soon someone next door started to pound on the wall. So the man sat on the floor with the dog and just acted calm and friendly until the dog left off his booming and sank the few inches onto his belly.

That's when the second rattle came at the door. A cheeping sound like a distant cricket. The man went and opened and there was a parakeet in a cage at the sill and on the cage a note saying, "Take care of me." There was this marvelous green thing flapping inside the cage from bar to grill to bar in fright. And the man could still smell the fresh air left by the person who put the cage there, someone now lost in the crowd outside.

He picked up the cage and brought it in for the SPCA in the morning. "They'll really believe me," he thought. The cage door had not been shut tight. It swung open as he put it down on his hall table, so the parakeet flew out and all over the room, zooming by the dog's head a few times, so the dog began to bark his deep, mournful barks again, the wall began to pound, and the man began to laugh.

He calmed the dog with a sausage from the fridge and let the parakeet stay loose, bopping into mirrors and pictures until it finally settled on his bust of Homer over the old fireplace.

Then he heard what he thought were the sounds of a cat outside the door. "Geez," he thought, and he opened it, and there was a baby wrapped up like a papoose on the threshold with a note saying, "I just had this, and I can't keep it." This wasn't funny. There was a woman out there who had given birth alone and needed care. He checked the baby quickly. It was okay. The dog boomed and strained toward the open door. The man pulled the baby in and slammed the door quickly just as the parakeet went belting into the door and then rebounded back across the room and landed again on Homer's head.

The man got on the phone to the police, who said they would come as quick as they could, what with the crowds in the streets and all the extra duty. So he told them to get on TV and radio and tell that mother go get a check-up quick. The hospitals were open. No questions asked. Just go.

The police said, "Yeah," and the man hung up just in time to hear the sound of running water up against his door. He thought it was someone taking a leak and he wasn't about to jerk open the door to find out. "Somebody left the damn downstairs unlocked," he thought. But the water kept going. It would have to be an elephant. So he opened the door a crack and saw water coming off the corridor ceiling.

There was a woman halfway down the stairs in her night clothes and curlers who said to him, "It's okay, it's okay, a sink over-flowed, water'll stop in a minute."

The parakeet hit the door again and the dog woof–woofed and the baby began to cry. That startled the woman, so she said, "I'll get a mop," and she hopped up the stairs in loose slippers. So the man went back and soothed the dog and patted the baby. The par-akeet landed on his head.

There was a knock on the door this time. It was a timid knock, not cops, not the lady with the mop. The man went to answer it, with the parakeet on his head and the dog booming woofs and the baby crying but weakly like a new one. He opened the door and knew it was the mother. By some miracle the parakeet didn't fly out and the dog stopped barking to look at this new creature.

"It's mine," the woman said. "I just can't leave it."

"Come right in here," the man said, "and sit. I'm going to call and get someone to come. You gotta have care."

He was on the phone, through to the police. "I want an ambulance. I want it now." And he explained why.

"Yeah," said the police, "soon as we can."

As he hung up there was another rap at the door, this time not so timid. The dog really let loose, the parakeet went crazy, from the man's head to Homer's head, back to his, quick as green lightning. The man opened the door and knew it was the dog's owner standing there—a little old lady as frail as bone china.

"I couldn't hold him," she said, "he drags me downstairs and upstairs and out into traffic. But I can't surrender him."

The dog was delirious with booming joy, prancing on his sparkplug legs.

"Let him calm down," said the man. "Then you can manage. Here, sit with this kid. It's her baby. I think she had it herself."

The old woman was afraid of the young woman and wouldn't sit near her, but mumbled, then looked around, took the leash while the dog slobbered all over her, made for the door, and once outside it seemed to take off like a motor bike pulled by a powerful engine.

The man got the mother some tea. She was the picture of depression. He looked at the baby. It needed cleaning. So he got a basin, took some warm water from the tap, some soap, stripped the baby, saw how much needed to be done, did a little by washing what he could, got a cotton blanket, started to wrap it, a boy child, just as another knock came at the door. His hands were full, so he shouted, "Come on in!"

It was a college student. She said her roommate had gotten rid of her parakeet because he didn't like it. And had finally said where he left it as she got rid of *him*.

"Right here," the man said, the bundle of baby still in his hands. "Look, just come and sit with this mother until the ambulance arrives. She had this herself and just showed up here. I'll catch the parakeet."

But the young woman was afraid also. Just then there was a great pounding on the stairs as the police and paramedics arrived. They moved in efficiently on the baby and the mother and on the man for the answers he knew and on the young woman who owned the parakeet but knew nothing.

It was a while before they all cleared out and left the man standing in the middle of a mess. The TV showed the ball descending, twenty-five seconds, twenty seconds, ten, five, midnight! Happy New Year! "Should auld acquaintance be forgot . . ."

The dog had dropped one near the radiator. There was a dirty diaper left behind. The parakeet had left its mark on Homer's head. There was still a puddle of water near the door. The man saw some traces of blood on the cushion where the mother had sat. And a funny thing happened to him. He felt a love of life well up in him until it was like an ecstasy. Then it passed. He spent an hour cleaning up, then he turned on music, sat in the chair where the woman had sat, ate his cold cuts, bread and beer, then said to himself, "Next year I go out, where it's safe."

11. Drumming Up Christmas

For the Second Sunday after Christmas

> Out of his full store we have all received grace upon grace; for while the Law was given through Moses, grace and truth came through Jesus Christ.
>
> JOHN 1:16–17

There was a man who played kettle drums for the symphony. The rhythm of drums explained the whole world to him. Everything had a beat. He remembered the night his first daughter was born. His wife was the drummer. She had turned the slow rhythms of pain into the larger pulses of new life, then into the slow beat of peace. He went home that night to the soft tap of her love.

He had three daughters now. His wife really couldn't play a note. She took what he said on faith. Every now and then she'd flip a switch on the stereo and ask "Who?" And he'd say "Beethoven, Violin Concerto, first four beats!"

Christmas night he had to read the birth of Jesus to them all, out of the King James Bible. She wanted it because it was a tradition in her family.

"We're all girls," she said, "so you have to follow my family."

But he couldn't just read. When the oldest was nine and could, he had her read it. And he set up everything he could get a beat from. She would read a line and he would play, kettle drum, marimba, gourds, gong, snare drum, chimes, even the musca that buzzed like a fly.

The girls couldn't stay passive so they began to take over instruments and pretty soon he had a tympany orchestra. People outside the house couldn't hear the reading of the Christmas story from Luke, but they could hear everything you could beat with a stick. All improvised.

"Okay read," he said, and began the soft stroke as though an Indian drum, a tom tom, or a jungle drum on a moonless night.

"And while they were there the time came for her to be delivered."

The eight-year-old began to tap the chimes softly.

"And she gave birth to her first born son."

The seven-year-old hit the chinese gong a mighty stroke with a mallet almost as big as she, then collapsed on the couch with a grin bigger than big. The man shifted the rhythm on the kettle drums to a soft jazz, like something looking to be fixed.

"She laid him in a manger because there was no place for them in the inn." His wife began to brush the snare drum with soft strokes.

"There were shepherds out in the field keeping watch over their flocks by night."

"Baa, baa," went the nine-year-old with a gourd.

"Boom, boom, baboom, boom, boom," went the man on the bass drum.

And the seven-year-old hit the gong a mighty stroke and fell over again on the couch.

"And an angel of the Lord appeared to them."

"Chime, chime, ring, ring," went the eight-year-old and her mallet.

"Pling, plung, plang, chong," went the wife on the marimba. And the man rained his mallets lightly on the high kettle as if there were feet overhead.

"Gagong," went the seven-year-old who was now out of the story completely and into a world of her own.

Just then the doorbell buzzed. And it buzzed as if someone meant it. The nine-year-old put down the Bible and ran out the hallway to the front door. There were four young people there in punk dress and they scared the nine-year-old so she ran back in the parlor and left the door open.

The four punks came around the corner and saw the whole tympany equipment of a symphony orchestra jammed into the parlor space, saw the Bible the nine-year-old clutched and the square-looking man and square-looking wife and they said "Geez! We thought somethin' good was happenin'!"

The man started a soft beat on his drums, a rare beat only someone on drugs would know, "da boom boy, boy ba ba da," and he increased it slowly, moving through the three drums like a train across three switches. And the punks stood there because he was using only his hands and he looked straight at them.

They knew he was reading them. He read one kid's Indian war lock, another's dagger earrings, another's patched jeans. Then he slowed to a waking up rhythm and he said to his nine-year-old, "Please read."

And she started at, "And this will be a sign to you, you will find a babe wrapped in swaddling cloths and lying in a manger."

The punks made terrible faces and backed out of the room like the Marx brothers and roared laughter as they hit the front steps. Crazy, crazy.

The woman got up, closed the door and came back. All the rhythms had stopped. So she said to the nine-year-old, "Please read more."

"Glory to God in the highest and on earth peace among men with whom he is pleased."

And the man began again, still with his hands, African style, making the sounds of wings, a light stroke, then a caress, then snapping his fingers lightly on the skins to make the plucking of strings sound, like random starlight. Then the light drumming of feet over the earth to the stable.

And the nine-year-old read, "And they went with haste and found Mary and Joseph, and the babe lying in a manger."

And the seven-year-old hit the gong for all she was worth and fell over in ecstasy on the rug. And that shook everybody into action so they all played a joy on something until even the house began to creak.

Then the buzzer sounded again. This time the mother went to the door and faced a group of neighbors who said "This is a holy season and you're making a racket fit for hell. You'll ruin those children."

The smell of pot was in the air from the punks, so the neighbors intensified their complaints, saying they would call the cops and have the children taken. Just then the nine-year-old came into the hallway holding the Bible.

"It's a cult," said one of the group. That convinced them and they turned, intending to get the police.

The woman let them go. Police would go through a form, accept an explanation, then leave. She came back and she said to her husband, "Just softly." And to her nine-year-old, "Just the last few lines."

"And the shepherds returned glorifying and praising God for all they had heard and seen."

And he began to play, still with his bare hands, the rhythms of the carols. And they recognized each one. The seven-year-old was asleep under the gong. The eight-year-old was standing at the kettle drums guessing each carol with intensity a few bars into the rhythm. And the nine-year-old had reached a hand in and was following her father's beat on the outer edge of the drum which made a different sound.

And his wife who couldn't play a note picked up the seven-year-old, sagged at the knees, and went up the stairs to put her to bed. As she did, her husband changed the beat to "The Lark Ascending," a drum imitating a flute, just fingers on skin.

"Good," she said, "good, but she weighs a ton, this lark."

12. The Magi Mural

For Epiphany

In former generations this was not disclosed to the human race; but now it has been revealed by inspiration to his dedicated apostles and prophets, that through the Gospel the Gentiles are joint heirs with the Jews, part of the same body, sharers together in the promise made in Christ Jesus.
EPHESIANS 3:6

There was a man who knew that gifts corrupted people. But he had to give gifts to stay in business. He owned warehouses. So he used to give symphony tickets or passes to museums. But he got funny looks for that, from people who wanted tobacco and booze. What he did next was choose some rare wines. The kind no one in his right mind could chug-a-lug. He was stuck about tobacco. What he gave was rare incense from India, even though he knew it made an aroma which could cover the smell of pot.

He really wanted to give works of art by new artists, but they scared people silly. And people sold them on the sly for the money. He once bought the same painting twice, a few years apart, before he learned. And religious art, he thought religious art was fascinating. When it was good, it was very, very good. When it was bad, it was horrid.

One year he found a painting of the Magi he went ape over. In the painting, the Magi were three apes—human beings in three stages of development, as in anthropology books. A magnificent ape just beginning to walk upright, massive, marvelous shoulders and arms. He was reaching for a fat flower in a tree. Maybe to eat it. Maybe to smell it. The next was a hairy female, walking upright. She had a baby on her hip and a calabash on her head with fruit spilling out. She looked as if she had been pumping iron. The third was a tall, tall Masai with a black and beautiful body, the finished human being. The man was standing on one leg in a tribal posture, supporting himself on a beautifully carved ceremonial staff. He was taller than the mountain in the background. And there was a naked white modern woman with a naked white modern baby and a naked white modern man looking at the three magi and pointing with surprise and delight, as if they knew them. The white man had a monkey on his shoulder who gripped the man's head in terror. And there was a dog barking from around the woman's legs. The title of the painting was "Syzygy," written across the sky of the canvas in the shape of a megaphone in gold leaf.

"That's it!" said the man who was looking at the picture. "That's it for this year!"

So he bought it and got permission to make a fairly large photo reproduction of it, made many copies of that, and sent them out as gifts. No wine, no incense, just *Syzygies*. Well, his Christian customers threw a fit. His Jewish customers were too embarrassed to say a word. His nonbelieving customers thought he was starting a new magazine and was testing it out on them. His Zen customers thought he was missing the whole point. "I'll be lucky to stay in business," he thought. But very soon a woman showed up in his office dressed in paint-spotted jeans and jacket. Her eyes were almost popping with excitement.

"Can I paint that Magi thing on a wall in my neighborhood? Just a small wall."

"A brick wall?" the man asked.

"Yes," she said, "yes."

"It'll cause a riot!" the man said.

"No, it'll stop one," the woman said.

"You better see the artist," the man said.

"He says okay," she said, "but you own the painting."

"Okay by me," the man said, "but let me check it before you unveil it. It may not look good larger than it is."

"Oh, it'll look good," the woman said, and she practically ran out the door.

Six months of poor business went by for the man, and he was thinking of going back to booze and tobacco for next Christmas. Then he read in the paper one morning: "New Ad Raises Ire." And there was a picture of his painting. The wall was 200 feet long and 300 feet high. It was an old cold-storage warehouse. In fact he owned it. "What the hell?" he said. Then he saw another paper: "People Crazy For New Wall." Then another: "Wall Creates Folk Festival."

He skimmed down the column. Singers were showing up, street acrobats, organ grinders, hot dog carts, in the big lot next to the warehouse. Kids were throwing tomatoes and bottles, betting they could hit vital spots. Parents were chasing them away and taking mops on long poles and washing off the vital spots. And there were candles at night, some aloft on tethered balloons, so there was a marvelous flicker of light and shadow over all the figures in the painting. And the music bounced off the wall like a superball, the guitars, the banjos, the mountain fiddles. Nothing electronic was allowed—no need: the other walls nearby made a perfect sound box.

The cops were stunned. They had everything they needed— mace, water cannon, shields, billy clubs, horses who were prancing and dirtying the streets. But somehow people policed the scene themselves. There *were* arguments. People dragging their kids to see, people dragging their kids away. And taxis were roaring in with tourists, then parking up on sidewalks so the drivers could join the crowd. The scene didn't stop, though people came and went.

The phone began to ring in the man's office. Would he endorse "Syzygy" jeans and have them painted on the Magi? Would he endorse "Bric-a-brac" Bras and have them painted on the women? There were calls from shampoo companies, dog food companies, monkey wrench companies. The man's phone broke from being slammed down in anger. He got in a cab himself and went to look, saw his painting on the wall, fell in love with it all over again, but saw it was going to be too much for people to live with. There would soon be a riot.

He spotted the mural painter in a crowd of people; she was arguing with them to keep the painting as it was. But they were having none of it. Others were having all of it. The man knew the decision was his, even though no one knew he was there.

He went back to his office, picked up the phone, got the jeans company and said, "Okay, put jeans on them."

Then he called Bric-a-brac Bras and said, "Okay, bras for the two females."

Then he called the shampoo company, "Okay, heads with a halo of soap suds."

Then the dog food company, the monkey wrench company. And he called other companies, eyeglasses, suntan lotions, hair dryers. Last he called the booze and tobacco companies. Crews began to show up the next day, lowering scaffolds down from the roof and painting in their products. The whole scene changed from a folk festival to an open air market where the products were sold, people coming from all over to buy them. And the man made a fortune from the rents and royalties. People began to look on him as a business genuis.

The door of his office opened one day and the paint-spattered woman came in and sat down.

"You owe me something," she said.

"Yes," he said. "I'll write you a check for half of what I made." She didn't move. She just sat there in the chair.

"Or I have another big warehouse and you can have the wall."

"But you'd chicken out again," she said.

"I didn't chicken out," he said. "They couldn't take it and you know it."

"I want to paint Jesus," the woman said. "Jesus crouched on a surf-board under the curve of a perfect wave. He'll have holes in him and wear a crown of thorns. And the wave will be missiles curving down to explode on his head and outstretched arms."

"What about the surfboard?" the man said.

"Oh," she said, "That'll be a woman's body stretched out like a diver, and he'll be balanced between her buttocks and shoulders."

"Take the check," the man said.

"No," she said. "I want that wall."

13. Off the Tracks

For the First Sunday in Ordinary Time

> He will tend his flock like a shepherd
>   and gather them together with his arm;
> he will carry the lambs in his bosom
>   and lead the ewes to water.

ISAIAH 40:11

There was a man who drove a trolley for a living. Half of each trip was on the surface, half underground. The underground was hardest for him to take—rails, walls, platform, rails, walls, platform. He had to announce each stop like a robot to robots.

One day something slipped into his voice at the first underground stop. "Kenmore Square. Now Bamboozle Square. There's a bookstore here that sells you baloney and a pizza joint that sells you cardboard."

People heard just words, they didn't understand what. They got ready to leave the streetcar and take the one behind, thinking this one was broken. But the doors closed, the brakes hissed, the car glided forward. The driver was happy. He didn't know what had got into him either.

At the next stop he said, "Auditorium. Really whistle, piss, and argue. Watch out for the bums, the rock and roll, the symphony, the squash balls."

Some people caught on and thought he was nuts. He might drive this street car off the tracks. Others caught on and looked at each other for the first time. Some got mad at the vulgarity and drew themselves up. The doors closed, the brakes hissed, the car glided forward, the driver grinned, down the rails, the walls, the dark tunnel until the next stop.

"Copley," he said over the speaker. "Lose your wallet/lose your mind/pray to God/for them to find."

People knew. The public library took hours to bring you a book. The mall took seconds to lift your cash. And there were churches left and right that were built by the old merchants. A lot of people got off, and a lot of people got on who sensed something in the people still on board. Doors closed. Brakes hissed. Car glided forward.

The man picked up the mike and started to sing softly to the tune of "Oh Tannenbaum," "Arlington, Oh Arlington, we come into your station. Thy Ritz is full. Thy park is fun. Thy buses stink. Thy noses run. Arlington, Oh Arlington, we come into your station."

People were getting mad for being interrupted this way. Some rattled the pages of their newspapers. High school kids started some raucous catcalls to take the scene over for themselves. But some people loved the guy and were looking around at each other with a new freedom. Riders got off, riders got on.

The car left the station. As it screeched around a curve, the man went on the mike, "Boylston, Boylston, where the fortune cookie crumbles, and the hard core rumbles, and the alkie stumbles, and the actor bumbles, and the doctor fumbles for the things he leaves inside you. Boylston, Boylston, better stay on."

"Say some good things about a place," a voice called from down the packed car.

"Park St. coming up," said the driver over the mike. "Goody State House, Goody Chapels, Goody bargain basements and a Goody Bible Belt."

This was a main stop so nearly everyone got off. Just a few got on for the run to Haymarket and a turnaround. So the man announced no more than the station, spoke like a robot to robots, then watched the tracks, the walls, the platform as if the voice had abandoned him and left him like a mole.

"End of mole hole, everybody off," he said when he had stopped the trolley.

After it was empty, he closed the doors and pulled into the tunnel where he was to reverse the car in a loop for the return trip, then wait for the signal to reenter the station outbound.

Someone moved across the aisle from behind him to where she could be seen. She had a slip of paper in her hand. She reached it toward him with some diffidence. He knew she couldn't speak English. The paper said Kenmore. His "Bamboozle Square." She had missed it. His baloney had confused her.

"Seven stops from here," he said to her, and held up seven fingers, then pointed ahead through the tunnel.

She moved somewhat fearfully toward the door, thinking he was parked there for good.

"No, no," he said, "sit, sit, there where I can see you. I'll tell you where to get off."

She didn't know what to do. So he got out of his seat and backed her into one just next to the door and said, "Wait there until I tell you."

And he held his two hands out like an orchestra conductor softening a sound. Then he put his two hands on his chest, then pointed to his mouth, then stretched his hands toward her ears, then pointed ahead, then touched his watch, then pointed to the door. She got up and started toward it as if he was saying lunchtime, be over in an hour.

"No, no," he said, "No!" Then he pointed to his head as if to say "Tonto."

She thought he meant her and he did. So she blushed angrily and sat down like a scolded pupil. He sat down and looked at her from his seat, and seven times he moved his hand in a wait signal, like a cop. Then the eighth time, he pretended to blow a whistle, and waved his hand toward the door. She seemed to understand. And her own hands began to move. The signs came quickly and beautifully to tell him she was thankful from her heart for his help to her who was in a foreign city to meet a friend who was to take her to a hospital for treatment of the deaf.

The guy was amazed that he understood, not all of it, but enough. Why had she not understood him? Maybe she thought he was saying he had no time or patience to tell her where to get off. "I better not make any more of my signs," he thought. "She'll get the opposite of what I mean. I want to hug myself and point to her to tell her how much I like her. She'll think I want to do something." But he did point to his head in the "Tonto" sign and pointed to his heart to tell her he was stupid about all this. She blushed and smiled and sat back at ease as if she were trusting herself to someone's head and heart.

The green light went on outside the car, telling him to start outbound. He didn't want to. He wanted to stay and learn how to talk to this woman. But she had a stop to make. And he was to tell her which one.

So he eased the car forward and said aloud to himself, "Haymarket. There's no hay here. But there's a market. It's for yuppies. Their bite is worse than their bark. So wear gloves." He opened the doors and riders poured on.

He closed the doors and said, "Park next, Park."

14. Oysters, Tabasco, and Flies

For the Second Sunday in Ordinary Time

On the third day there was a wedding at Cana-in-Galilee.

JOHN 2:1

A man and a woman were eating oysters on the half-shell at the No-Name Restaurant on the Fish Pier and she said to him, "Well, that's it, twelve empty shells!"

"No," he said, "two full bellies, what an anniversary! I'm as pregnant as you are!"

"Oh you poor dear," she said, "I'll have to be super-nice to you now!"

"No," he said, "just oysters on the half-shell every week, at No-Name, after mass. I'll be okay, I'll get through, one more year."

"Of me!" she said.

"No, of mass," he said, "you're a feast. You're better than oysters on any fish pier."

"How many years can you get through with me?"

"There aren't any years with you. It's all a split second, a thrill

like a split second, a catch in the end zone, a slap shot to beat the
clock, oh, oh, oh, what a feeling, Toyota!"

"They're looking at you," she said. "Imagine singing a commer-
cial to a pregnant wife!"

"Maybe they don't think 'wife,'" he said. "Maybe they think
'wild girl friend,' live-ins!"

"A toothpaste ad," she said, "comfy sex kids."

"They're looking at you. They're turning into Knights of the
Round Table. You asked for tabasco and we've got twelve here on
the table. They fell into the sauce, see, like flies!"

"Those are flies, or something!"

"This isn't very spiritual, oysters, tabasco, and flies."

"Well, I love this treat," she said. "I love being here with you,
and I did drag you to church for your soul, so you'd remember one
happy mass."

"Today's wasn't too bad," he said, "I like that wedding feast
story, those pots had more than wine in them when the Lord got
through. They were like pregnant women, people got drunk on
beauty, like me here looking at you."

"I didn't think you heard a word. I thought you were mesmer-
ized by me!"

"Well, you see, I'm the kind of guy who can do two things at the
same time, love that feast and love that you."

"It was more than wine, wasn't it?" she said. "He was giving
himself away and she knew it, she asked him to. You remember
how you gave your father that kiss as we were leaving the hall, he
was so full he couldn't move."

"I remember," he said, "I'd never kissed anyone but you. Now
I go around kissing lamp posts and pay checks and parking
tickets, see what you've done. I'm even kissing these oysters
before I swallow them alive!"

"That wedding was so beautiful," she said. "It's as if everything
turned holy because of it."

"In that reading today at mass?" he asked.

"No, at ours," she said. "Well, I mean at ours too, even the cake
was sacred. I kept licking my fingers, the words we said were like

a scent all over everything, there was a glow and it wasn't alcohol. I loved every second as if it was holy and was going to stay that way."

"It has, hasn't it!" he said. "Twelve months and we're still high on one feast!"

"Do you think that's what life is really like?" she asked, "a bride, a groom?"

"I think it is," he said, "and I think it isn't, people can't take the beauty."

"But we can."

"Oh, yes," he said, "we can, because I'm Tarzan and you're Jane, but they can't, and if we don't order something else or leave, that crowd at the door is going to stare us into perdition."

"Well," she said, "the Lord said love would be misunderstood."

"Yes, but I say we've been overcharged."

15. My Keeper's Brother

For the Third Sunday in Ordinary Time

> He began to speak: "Today," he said, "in your very hearing this text has come true."
>
> LUKE 4:21

A man volunteered to be a missionary to an African people. "Go there and learn everything about them before you say a word," they told him. "If you want to come home at any time, just let us know and we'll have you out."

So the man went there and took years to learn the complicated language. Then he learned their stories about the creation of the world, about the fall from original creation, about the repair of it, and finally about the destiny of the two souls each person had, one back into the people as a force to help them live, one back to the creating god as a force to help that god live. He learned their art, their dance, their ways of marriage, their ways of trade, their ways of settling conflicts. He was good at agriculture, so during all this time he earned his way by helping to cure the crops they had, by increasing the yield, and by showing safe ways to store surplus foods.

Finally, after fifteen years, he sent a message saying, "I want to come home." Within a few days his ticket arrived. People knew he was to leave, though he had said nothing. On the day of his departure everyone was standing in silence near their huts and along the paths from the cliffs down to the dirt road that the bus used to cross the country between the major places. The silence was absolute, but filled with feeling—love, respect—something like that. There was no sadness. There was a kind of joy. The man felt it but did not understand. He caught the bus in the morning and by evening was on a small plane which would take him to a larger plane which would take him home. Some days later he went to church headquarters to report and to say why he had asked to leave.

He said, "They have a faith. It fits them. And mine does not. So I never said a word. I had to leave or convert to their ways."

The church leaders said, "Well, would they accept another man?"

"Yes, Oh yes!" he said, and he told about the rare event of his leaving.

"And what will you do now?" they asked.

"I want to relearn Christianity," he said.

They said goodbye to each other, and the man went out to relearn. He relearned first the doctrines of creation, and spent many nights in wild arguments about how God did it, in six days fossils and all, or slowly with big bangs and genetic leaps, or like the maker of a clock. Then he relearned the doctrines of the fall, and spent many days in the crossfire between those who believed in the total corruption of the world, or who believed we were all just tainted, or who said we pick it up like a cold from the common chinaware we use. And some said it's metaphor, just try hard and things change for the better.

Then he relearned the doctrines of redemption. And it was like facing a massive thunderstorm, lightning flashing divine anger down on a brutalized human hulk pinned to a cross. Or a man carrying a sheep under attack from wolves. Or a game of political chess and one man gets to save a few pieces.

And finally he relearned the doctrines of where the soul goes. To many kinds of hell, to many kinds of purgatory, to one kind of heaven. During all this time he supported himself by teaching about the African tribe he had studied.

The day came when he knew he had relearned Christianity. And his relearning had reduced him to silence.

One day the church called him. It was puzzled. The new man they sent out to take his place was learning nothing. However hard he tried people would instead ask to learn his language, and then his myths, creation, fall, redemption, destiny. They helped him do his chores, showed him ways to improve his living under their hard conditions. No one joined his belief, but everyone seemed to know it, and in his words, not in their own tongue. They were absolutely silent about themselves. And when anyone came or went from the village they all stood in silence and the air was filled with a respect, a love, that was extraordinary.

The new man didn't know what to do. In fact the people were going to neighboring tribes and mastering their beliefs. And the neighboring tribes thought there was some evil afoot, under the guise of good.

So the church said to the first man, "What did you do to them? You have kept them from becoming anything even as they try to become everything."

A deep feeling of hurt came over the man.

"They are something," he said. "That is why they can learn from someone else."

"Shall we call the new man home?" they asked him.

"Yes," he said, "they understand all he has to give."

The first man left church headquarters. He felt a strange ecstasy come over him. It was as if he saw Christ and Christianity for the first time. "Christ is like a restorer of works of art," the man thought. "His knowledge of things must be exquisite before he touches them. And after he touches them they are what they were, if they have any substance at all. And if they have little or none he can tell the story of what they were. And no one knows he did it. And that is what he made me on my tiny scale."

But then the man paused in his walk, a doubt coming over him. "I can't make Jesus responsible for every good thing that happens in the world. That takes goodness away from people who do not know him and yet do miracles to save what they can save."

His ecstasy died down. He was near some shops. One of them was a pet shop. There was a macaw in the window, several cages of canaries, and two monkeys who had their arms wrapped around each other for comfort. He remembered the cartoon of the two monkeys in the Philadelphia Zoo, the one saying to the other, "You mean to say that I'm my keeper's brother?" It was still funny. And these two monkeys came to the glass and tried to get through as if to grab him for comfort. So he pressed his face softly to the glass as if to become a monkey too, and they rubbed their heads against the glass thinking they were rubbing him. But they weren't fooled for long. There was a barrier. "Maybe that's it," he thought. "There's a place where Jesus has to stop. And everyone else begin."

16. Ruckus in the Spice Aisle

For the Fourth Sunday in Ordinary Time

Brace yourself, Jeremiah;
stand up and speak to them.
Tell them everything I bid you,
do not let your spirit break at sight
    of them,
or I will break you before their
    eyes.

JEREMIAH 1:17

There was a woman who was old. Everyone she loved was gone. It had just happened that way. She had a dog who loved her, but she knew the difference. She was still active and looked for ways to relate. One way was to go shopping for a trifle like pepper in a supermarket. That meant getting on a bus for the elderly and being delivered to and fro. There were a lot of dead-end people on that bus, but it was a chance to share the weather and aches and pains and the number of pills between being up or down.

Inside the supermarket was another story. She would go down the spice aisle, find the pepper section which was out of her reach, then ask whoever came by to reach up and help her make a selection. On the weekdays it was the women, often with their babies riding the carts, and the old woman got to see all kinds, fat, thin, cranky, calm. Babies and mothers. Often the mother would say, "What do you want it for?" And the old woman would launch into a description of spaghetti with melted butter that needed a good sprinkling of black pepper to make it really come alive.

Usually the mother would be highly amused at an old woman who would even think of generously seasoning food, never mind making such a tasty plate. So there'd be some recipe swapping, and talk about the baby, and what the husband could take and could not. Never more than five or ten minutes. But a delicious conversation for the old woman.

On Saturdays she met the men. She had to choose something

other than pepper. Vinegar this time. Not any old vinegar. Up out of reach. And she'd ask a man to reach a bottle down to her so she could look at it, and she wondered aloud if this would be right for romaine lettuce and artichoke hearts minus the anchovies because she hated the fish taste. And often the men would say use any old kind and she would say any old kind was what killed her love for salads. Which she needed or the jig would be up for her. Then they'd find out how old she was and how she had no one and making a meal was like a ritual, for if anyone came back from the dead she would still know how to prepare a meal, the way Hasidic Jews kept a plate for the Messiah who mostly came for a handout so no one knew he came and the place was always set.

Usually the men liked this, listening to a crazy old lady chatter mystically, they had a sense of taking care of something, a bird with a broken wing. And the old woman could sense that, so she would choose a vinegar and let the man go, though often the men would say how long it had been since they had seen their mothers.

One day she was in the market looking for butterscotch pudding and saw it up out of reach. She looked around for help, but there was only a pregnant woman pushing a two-year-old in a cart. The pregnant woman seemed to be in trouble, no more than a few feet away. She seemed to turn inward, then outward again.

She saw the old woman standing there, and she simply said, "Please," and began to lower herself to the floor as the two-year-old looked at her with growing fright.

The old woman knew the other woman could have the baby right on the spot. So she moved as quickly as she could to the check-out lines and beckoned to the cashier to come, but the cashier was busy and didn't move, so she said to anyone in line, "Come help someone who may be giving birth," and she turned and shuffled back up the aisle to where the woman was lying on the floor, nearly concealed behind her shopping cart.

No one came, so the old woman grabbed three or four packages of pudding, went to the head of the aisle again, and began to throw them one by one at the cashiers.

They looked up and said, "Hey, cut it out, lady!"

"Then you come!" she said. "Somebody needs you!"

The cashiers started looking around for the manager because they could not leave their posts, and the customers didn't want to leave their lines or their carts. So the old woman reached for a bottle of Mouton Cadet Rothschild, and she smashed it on the floor, six bucks' worth of wine marked down to four.

"She's nuts," someone said.

So she smashed another one and a cry went up from the cashiers for the manager, who came out of his booth at the end of the store near the exit wondering what all the ruckus was.

The cashiers were pointing like mad at the woman at the head of an aisle as she raised another bottle of wine over her head and smashed it on the floor. The manager started to move quickly toward the old woman. As soon as she saw him, she moved back down the aisle toward the pregnant woman who was in trouble. The manager rounded the corner on the double and there were the two, the young and old woman. He understood the situation, and he did not want it.

"I'll get you a cab," he said. "If you can just get up, we can go out the side door and get you a cab off to a doctor's." The manager didn't want anyone born in one of his aisles.

"You go phone for a doctor," the old woman said, "or I will tear this place apart with my bare hands."

"Just shut up, lady," the manager said.

"No," she said, "no."

She shuffled back to the head of the aisle where she shouted in her weak voice, "A doctor! A doctor! A nurse! A nurse!"

There was a nurse in line who sensed the call was real. So she left her purchases at the counter, threaded back through the line, and disappeared down the aisle.

She looked at the woman and said, "She's close. It'll be here or in somebody's car."

The old woman ran back down the aisle. Now everyone was watching the head of the aisle. And she reappeared, shouting in her weak voice, "A station wagon, a station wagon to have a baby."

A man left the line immediately, pulling his teenage son by the arm to follow.

In the aisle the nurse said, "Lift her. I'll take the baby. You, manager, show us the side door. Is your car close?" she asked the man and his son.

"It will be in two seconds," the man said and handed the keys to the son, who shot down the aisle, high-jumped the turnstile and was out the door lickety-split.

The manager and the man helped the woman, the nurse held the two-year-old, and in a slow walk they all went to the side door, then out where the son had the car ready.

They drove off, leaving the manager to pull the door shut behind him. The old woman was standing there looking.

"Someone has to pay for that wine," she said. "The pudding didn't get hurt."

"Just go away," he said.

"Walk me away," she said. "Or I'll get hit with the bill."

"I'll let you out here," he said.

"No you won't," she said. "You walk me through the line or I'll tear this store apart with my bare hands."

"If you weren't a little old lady, I'd toss you out of here on your head," the manager said, though with some sense of the ridiculous beginning to dawn on him.

"If I weren't a little old lady," she said, "I'd give you a free ride to the moon."

17. Gambling Fever

For the Fifth Sunday in Ordinary Time

> And now, my brothers, I must remind you of the gospel that I preached to you; the gospel which you received, on which you have taken your stand, and which is now bringing you salvation. Do you still hold fast the gospel as I preached it to you? If not, your conversion was in vain.
>
> 1 CORINTHIANS 15:1–2

A young man was hitchhiking back to the East Coast. He had just finished graduate school. He had a job to go to, but he loved the open road and places along it. He took buses at night and thumbed during the day. Early in the trip he stopped at Tahoe. It was a glorious area, Tahoe, Truckee river, trees, mountains, sky. There was a church with a glass wall behind the altar and the whole lake spread out beyond the pines. And there were casinos. He'd never been in one.

"Ten dollars worth," he said to himself, and went in, got the coins, and walked up to a one-armed bandit and said, "Draw, you varmint!"

He put the coin in and hit a jackpot for one hundred dollars, the coins spitting out like chiclets onto the tray, onto the carpet where they wheeled around and crashed into his shoes. He grinned around at those who were happy he'd won, picked up the coins, a lot of weight, got a small bag from a woman attendant, and went looking for another machine. He found one, put a coin in, hit a jackpot, and a thousand silver dollars came pouring out like wheat from a bin.

This time he really needed help, not just the attendant with a larger canvas bag. People chipped in, scooping up the silver into the bag, and there was a terrific camaraderie. People actually began to rub him for luck. Which he loved.

He took the bag and exchanged the coins for paper money. But he kept a few coins and headed for another machine. People followed him now, and when he hit another jackpot for another thousand there was a small scene, people slapping thighs and backs and giving raucous laughs, scooping up coins for him, leaving him alleyways to any machine he liked. He hit ten straight jackpots—for ten thousand silver dollars, which he turned into paper money when the sacks got too heavy. People really began to rub him for luck. There was a frenzy around him. He saw their eyes afire with the itch to win. They went to machines beside him and threw money in frenetically, yet drew nothing.

He himself could feel the itch. So he said to the crowd, "I gotta take a leak," and headed for the toilet. Once inside he took a look at himself in the mirror and saw a crazed face, his hair standing on end, his cheekbones red, his mouth half open, and his tongue like a panting dog's.

"Stop, buddy," he said to himself. "No, more than stop! Get rid of this stuff!" He combed his hair down, threw cold water in his crazed face, composed himself, and left unobtrusively, changing the remaining coins into paper.

Out on the street he looked for a bank. He saw one, looked like a local, had a western saloon front to it, and inside nice brass ashtrays as big as the old spitoons.

He walked in and went up to a woman teller and said, "Can you give me a check for this ten thousand dollars?"

"Yes," she said, "made out to whom?"

"I don't know," he said. "A charity?"

"Which one?" she asked.

"I can't think," he said, "there are so many."

"You just won this, didn't you?" she said.

"You wouldn't believe it," he said, "ten plays, ten jackpots. I had a crowd. It's like we all had a fever."

"How about a hospital?"

"Yes."

"The Shriners run hospitals for burn victims," she said.

"Say, you're shrewd," he said.

"No. I know someone who was cared for by them when she was little. You know, kids and kerosene and matches in the back yard when mommy isn't looking. They did a magnificent job with her."

"Okay, Shriners. Where?"

"San Francisco. I'll give you a bank envelope, and I have the address."

"You give too, don't you?"

"Yes, but not ten thou."

Then he stopped and looked at her more closely, the high collar with the Matt Dillon string tie, the long sleeves to the wrist, perfect skin on her face, but a hint of ridges beginning at her collar line. She blushed a little.

"How bad?" he asked.

"Not too, I skip the beauty contests. And have to stay out of the sun. But I'm better than most statues left outdoors."

"I'd love to see," he said.

"Well thanks," she said, "a lot of people wouldn't."

"You married?" he asked.

"No, not yet," she said.

"Got anybody?" he asked.

She looked a little invaded, but answered, "No, just what's out there, rich man, poor man, beggar man, thief. All beating the door down."

"Will you marry me?" he asked.

She paused, for several minutes, looking at him, then looked down and very quietly arranged the numbers ten thousand on the money machine, inserted the blank check and pushed the button. The machine buzzed importantly. Then she took the check, inserted it in the envelope, wet the flap and sealed it, wet a stamp and put it on the corner, and addressed the envelope to the Shriners hospital. Then, still very quietly, she placed the envelope on the counter before the young man, but left her hand palm down on it and towards him.

"Yes," she said. "After you mail this."

18. Earth Mother

For the Sixth Sunday in Ordinary Time

These are the words of the Lord:
A curse on the man who trusts in
    man
and leans for support on human
    kind,
while his heart is far from the Lord! . . .
Blessed is the man who trusts in the
    Lord,
and rests his confidence upon him.

JEREMIAH 17:5-7

There was a woman who lived in a high valley in Bolivia. She had a family, a husband and two small girls. He worked the land so they had enough to eat and to trade. She did loom work, made alpaca sweaters which she sent down for sale to a co-op in one of the lower valleys. The designs were her own. The came out of her memory somewhere, from legends her parents had told her.

This life came to an end when her husband was killed in a truck accident. Truck was used as a bus. It didn't make a curve because its brakes failed and it pitched 3,000 feet into a gorge. She had gone down with the others and carried the bodies back up to the high valley where a priest said a mass. Instead of burying him with the rest she asked her brother to help her bring the body higher, up into a break in the mountain wall where a path went over and out toward the sea far away, an offshoot of the Inca trail. She and her brother buried her husband under a pile of rocks well off the trail, but looking down the westward slope to the lower mountains, toward the cloud bank that meant the sea. She left no marker, no cross, no anything, only the stones mounded like clothes on a baby on the cold nights back home.

She returned to her place and soon saw she would have nothing to live on. Her brother knew this too and told her to give up the loom work, it brought in too little, to give up trying to farm her own food, to put in coca plants instead. He would help her sell the leaves and that would make her a good life for herself and her own. So she told the co-op there would be no more sweaters, they could come and take the loom, which they did. She herself went into the fields with the coca seedlings she got from her brother and she put them in where the vegetables had been. But then she decided to put in vegetables every other row, on the chance she might need extra food.

It was a backbreaking season for her. Several times she had to carry in water, in skin bags, to keep the plants alive. The sun was life, but it dried things. On cold mornings she would stand outside against the wall of her home with her two girls and just let the rays penetrate through her clothing, through her skin, and reach her blood, which seemed to thaw and move into her fingers and toes like some force of resurrection.

The moon was death. Toward the end of the growing season she had to walk the fields most nights to keep others from cutting out the coca leaves. She had an old gun. She could use it. She had gone into the local village one day with it in the crook of her arm and a clay pot with nothing in it on her head. She set the pot on an odd shaped stone in the middle of the street, a stone no one moved because it was thought the Incas put it there to keep an evil force below ground, the force that made the earth shake. She walked some distance from it, looked back to be sure no children were near, then she blew it apart with one shot from forty yards away.

The priest was furious at her. She told him it was just symbolic of what a force of nature had done to her, she was the empty pot, and the bullet was her husband's death, and God was the rifleman. The priest was even more angry and required her to pick up the pieces of the clay pot and put them back together with some glue as a symbol of what she could do in spite of disaster. So she did. No one but the priest was fooled. They all knew she could shoot. So she harvested what she had planted.

Then she and her brother packed the leaves for sale. And they carried them over mountain paths to a place where the cocaine was made, taking several days back and forth to deliver it all. They had to cross wild country where there was nothing to stop the wind or the sky. On the last trip back they carried large amounts of American dollars.

Now she had to go down to the lower valley and buy pesos with those dollars to conceal her source of income, and then buy the food she would need for the coming year. She came into the square where the black market in money took place, young men and women who did the runner work for the money-people raced after every car or person they thought wanted to sell dollars for pesos. She was soon surrounded, but she understood no Spanish. Finally one knew her tongue, a young woman in jeans jacket and trousers and American jogging shoes, but with a face like her own, minus the black bowler hat all her people wore. They agreed on a dollar/peso exchange, away from the crowd, around the corner of the Franciscan church. The woman reached under her many skirts and brought out her packets of dollars. The runner pulled out huge pre-counted packets of pesos. The exchange took place.

The runner left, and the woman stored her pesos in her many skirts. She returned to the corner of the church ready to go purchase food. There she nearly stepped on a girl who was seated just around the corner, her back against the wall, her legs straight out in front of her, her chin on her chest, and her arms limp at her side. She was breathing. She was about fifteen. She was absolutely filthy, hair, skin, clothes, filthy beyond belief. And she was totally gone on cocaine.

The woman paused. She saw the young skin under the dirt. The sun would never touch that skin. A man would never touch that body except to rape it, and even then the girl would not know. The air of this place, thick with the fumes of exhaust and with dust from the dryness, would help to kill her. She would be dead soon because there was no way back for the thing she had become. And the woman felt the weight of the money in her skirts growing heavier, like the weight of a pregnancy, like the weight of her dead man whom she had buried up out of the reach of death against the sky. And she saw the filthy girl as what was born of this money. Then she saw herself and her own two girls starving to death without it. They needed the death of this girl or any other if their own lives were to go on. "I will live off one death," she said to herself. "But not another."

She went to a bank and with great difficulty, through an interpreter, put her money away, so she could return and draw on it each time she needed food, with each transaction marked in a small book she could not understand. She had put in a large amount. The bank thought she would bring more next year, and they treated her honestly so others from her village would come. During the long winter season she ate the one death. She saw the filthy girl again in different places but always in the same posture, until she never saw her again and knew she was buried in a field someplace with dogs and things that corrupted and caused harm.

The following year the woman refused the seedlings from her brother and put in vegetables. She got her loom back. And now she had to work night and day, risking the seasons, risking her own health, caring for the two girls, knowing there was very little between herself and starvation. "I will now live off my own death," she said. All around her people got richer and richer and she was a fool to them, to her own brother the biggest fool of all.

One day in the village where she went to trade food, she saw a girl leaning against the Inca stone, legs out in front of her, chin on her chest, her multiple skirts up like a turkey fan, her bowler hat fallen off so the part in her hair showed like a scar. She was drugged into insensibility, like the filthy girl from the valley. But this was a girl of the village. And she was dead, not asleep. So the woman went back quickly to her home, got her gun, and returned to the dead girl. By now everyone suspected there was a death. The woman proceeded to strip the girl of her clothing, she unbound her hair, and she laid the still warm but naked body over the stone so the body was like a crescent moon being carried on the back of some animal, feet down, hair down, belly and breasts to the sun.

As people approached the woman she waved the gun and said,

"You know I can use this!" And she put a shot by the priest to tell him he had no immunity. She walked around that body, and she sang a birth song they all knew, then she sang a wedding song they all new, then she sang a dirge they all knew. Then she shouted to them, "This girl stays here until you stop what killed her! This girl is you!"

She protected that body in the heat of the sun and the cold of the night until she herself was ready to drop and decomposition began. And the woman saw she was violating the corpse in another way. So she backed down the road and several men moved in quickly to take the corpse and clothing away. But something could not be taken away.

From then on flowers of some kind were always found on that stone. And when people died they were laid for a time on it though the priest had a fit. And some people were not rich anymore. And there was a mound of stones over the filthy girl's grave shaped like the wrappings of a baby in the cold of winter.

19. Back to the Stone Age

For the Seventh Sunday in Ordinary Time

Good measure, pressed down, shaken together, and running over, will be poured into your lap; for whatever measure you deal out to others will be dealt to you in return.

LUKE 6:38

There was a man who worked for Atomlab, a firm that designed nuclear weapons. It was attached to a larger complex that made the weapons, all within a five mile area, protected by a fence topped by barbed wire and heavily patrolled. It was in a lush valley between two ranges of hills, so whenever the man looked up from his work he saw a beautiful landscape leading up to sky that was always changing.

He was working on the design for the smallest possible nuclear weapon. The big bangs were making less and less sense. Precision was the word now: how to take out a building in a block and leave the block. No neutron stuff, that was outlawed. And minimum radiation. You didn't want to do in your own type. So design something on a rocket or a mortar shell. Or for open field fighting, use the cluster approach. That was what he was working on now—a cannister full of shotgun shells which would spray over an area like bird shot. But not to kill. The explosions were to take place several hundred feet above the ground and have the effect of concussion grenades, with the enemy stunned into immobility by the shock waves. And certain of the explosions would be aimed upward by the configuration of the shell, to lift the radiation above the field. The shock waves were what was wanted. The concept was neat.

He played with the designs on his computer screen like a geometrician first discovering geometry, reduplicating every possible situation and shifting his design so it would meet actual conditions before the first cluster was even made, never mind tested.

He was a divorced man. Not that his wife was anti-nuke. She was anti-abstract. He would look at her sometimes as if he had her on his screen and was revolving her to see if he couldn't improve her design. That was when she felt her nakedness as a shame. And she couldn't live with that. It was his daughter who was anti-nuke. His son was okay, though wavering. He played football and knew there were some healthy results to being tough.

His daughter had picked up her views at the state university, the same institution that produced most of the physicists he worked with. She was a biology major. That's what started it. She used to put a bowl of green leaves on the breakfast table the first day she was home from school. The next day one of the leaves would be reduced to a lace-like skeleton and so on through the whole bowl of leaves until there was nothing but skeletal shapes. She used nail polish to produce the effect.

"Why don't you just put a skull and crossbones on the table?" he had said to her one day.

"Because you're subtle," she said. "Halloween doesn't scare you."

He actually loved that answer. He was proud of her intelligence. Never mind what she was intelligent about. But she kept showing him the life his designs were intended to destroy. His wife had stopped all conversation between them. She used to feel bad about the leaves. She would often mount them in plastic and put them on the panes of the kitchen window so their beauty would show in the play of light.

Well, the three of them were gone. And he was doing what he had to do. Though he did love them more than any of his designs. The plant gate was regularly picketed by peace activists. He often had to ride through a forest of signs on his way in, signs telling him to quit, in God's name, in the earth's name, in the name of humankind, in the name of every name. Sometimes there were sit-ins, and the police had to haul the activists away, put them on buses and take them into town to charge them with obstruction. This day, a sit-in day, his wife and his daughter were there. The police were picking the two of them up fore and aft like rugs. He saw his daughter being lugged first, her shirt loose from her jeans and a stretch of skin showing, the blond skin he once had washed as if he were God with a new world. And then his wife. Her hair loose and dragging. She never loosened it, it was always combed close to her head and fastened in the back with a clip.

A horn beeped behind him. The road was clear. He drove in a few yards, made a U turn, drove out, went a mile, then pulled over and waited. The buses carrying the protesters came by, escorted by sirens and flashing lights. They were in there like school kids singing their way to a game or something. Up over their damn heads were satellites fixing on targets, so that when the enemy shot, the rockets would hit—and hit precisely. Would make skeletons out of them. No, would make them dark shadows on rocks. He whipped in behind the last cruiser and followed into town, to the courthouse.

The activists were lined up and led in. They looked like refugees. His wife and his daughter like two bums. Some people paid the fine and were let out on their own recognizance. They had other obligations and had made their protest. Some refused to pay and were sent off to a prison pen, to army huts in a field surrounded by a chain link fence, exactly like his place of work. That's where his wife and daughter ended up. And he sped out ahead of them to the prison gate, where he swung his car in front of it, across the entrance way, locked himself in, grabbed a notebook, and began to write signs and paste them up with tape inside the windows: "Fight big not little." "Send 'em home." "Get smart not tough."

The convoy pulled up. The police began to bang on his window, telling him to move it or they would. He refused.

"Pick on someone your own size," he shouted through the window. "Let 'em go, you *Gauleiter!*"

These were the harshest things he could think of. One of the police smashed the window across from him, unlocked the door and lunged in toward him. But the man shoved the keys in his pocket and held them there. The other door was unlocked, and the man was pulled struggling like an eel from the car.

"Fight an enemy, you bastards," he shouted.

They released the brake of his car and pushed it out of the way. They saw its decal. They knew he worked at the plant, the decal was mighty official. The buses then rumbled by into the pen and he saw the faces of his wife and daughter. And they saw him. His nose was a bit bloody and a cop was saying "Sorry!"

"Look, buddy," said the cop, "you lost your head. Go home and this didn't happen. They'll let 'em out in a few days, and in a month drop the charges. Cost too much to prosecute and they're not worth it. Just a nuisance."

"You sure?" said the man.

"It's all worked out," said the cop. "They know, we know, it's a game. The work goes on. This ain't Russia."

"I never had anything of mine put in jail," the man said. "Okay, I got to go to work. I can go?"

"Yeah," said the cop. "Just don't charge us for the window."

So the man left and drove back toward the plant. He felt like some kind of primitive beast that had fought a battle for its young. The emotions were still roaring inside him. His two, going by him in a bus, into a jail. He came to the entrance to the plant. It was clear. The gate was open. The security personnel smart-looking and alert. The fence in either direction neatly barbed and fierce-looking. He saw again the golden skin of the small of his daughter's back. He saw his wife's hair dragging on the pavement and dirt. He drove up to the security guards and showed them his pass.

"What's with the broken window?" one said.

"I locked myself out, couldn't get a wire in, had to break it."

He drove a few yards, then made a U turn and came back to the exit lane, then out a few yards, another U turn then back to the entrance way and the surprised security guards.

"No," he said. "I tried to picket a prison and the cops wouldn't let me. They busted the window and moved me out. My wife and daughter are in there. From here. That's what's with the window."

"Sir, you're upset. You can't go to work like this. Why don't you just go home and sleep in. They'll be back to you soon."

"No," the man said. "I'll have to go to them or it's nothing."

There was a polite beep behind him.

"Sir," said the guard, "please make a U and let these others enter."

"I can't see," said the man. His eyes were wet.

"Here, take a handkerchief, sir, I'll hold them for a minute. No, keep it, sir," the guard said. "I have another. Just swing around. And have a good day. We'll see you tomorrow."

20. Bishop's Dilemma

For the Eighth Sunday in Ordinary Time

Shake a sieve, and the rubbish
  remains;
start an argument and discover a
  man's faults.
As the work of a potter is tested in
  the furnace,
so a man is tried in debate.
As the fruit of the tree reveals the
  skill of its grower,
so the expression of a man's thought
  reveals his character.

ECCLESIASTICUS 27:4–6

"You don't lie," said the bishop to his prospective new secretary, "and you don't tell the truth. People get hurt by truths as much as by lies."

His maybe new secretary was green, he thought, unmarked by what really happens in this world.

The bishop continued, "I mean, suppose you have a scandal. A priest has been molesting altar boys. And the word comes in from someone who won't be named. So I send you to check it out discreetly and you find it's true. You don't tell people when I shift the priest. The damage to religion would be too great. You say the man is tired from the strain of his job and needs lighter duties in a parish up country. A few years there and he's ready for a heavy parish again. And you explain to those who really know that the man is under orders to get psychiatric help or we keep him away from everybody."

"What about criminal law?" said the new secretary. "Aren't you concealing a crime?"

"Yes and no," said the bishop. "People don't enter criminal complaints in church cases. And the law doesn't want to handle what could harm it. I mean a prosecutor doesn't want to put a priest in jail. That would threaten his career. If there's a complaint, I can't do a thing. If there isn't, I can do a lot."

"I don't want this job," said the green, maybe secretary.

"Incidents like that don't happen very often," said the bishop, "If you're squeamish, I'll handle it. But right now I need someone with a brain in his head. We've got issues coming at us like heavy traffic."

"What issues?" said the new man.

"Well, there's a former nun who converted to Episcopalianism. She went and got herself ordained by a bishop who was ordained a bishop by an Orthodox. Now she's here as university chaplain and people want me to say if she's a priest or not."

"You can just say no," said the new man.

"You catch on quick," said the bishop, "But if you just say no there's a furor in the community."

"So what do you say?" the new man asked.

"You say you'll ask Rome for a decision. You tell Rome there aren't many Orthodox here, so not to worry. But don't broadcast their decision."

"Meantime what?" the new man asked.

"Meantime you act if she is and isn't. You meet her as if she is, and you go to her services as if she isn't. I mean you appear at functions with her. If anybody asks, you are waiting for a Roman declaration, it's such a new problem."

"What do *you* think?" asked the new man.

"I think she probably is, but Rome will never admit it. I hear she's good."

"What else is headed at us?"

"Well," the bishop said, "there's the birth control stuff, and the divorce stuff, and now this gay stuff we're supposed to be hard line about. But we can't. We have to say one thing and do another. That's the straddle. With human sins you have to be soft as a grape. Even though Rome sends you a big stick. But the worst is this right wing, insisting on the purge of all impurity."

"You can't lie to them," said the man.

"No," the bishop said. "But you can distract them."

"How so?"

"You tell them you know things that will do their cause serious harm. So you can't press what they want you to press or facts will come out in the open and there's nothing you can do."

"Do you know facts?" asked the man.

"I don't," said the bishop. "But they do, and they get my point. One time there was a complaint about women preaching regularly in one of the parishes. It was close to the university. There were professors, really, with more degrees than I have rules. I find out the biggest complainer is ready to be canned by the school for his racist remarks in class and his techniques of harassment. So I hint that all the complainers might be tarred with the same brush. And I tell the pastor to have the women talk before or at the end of the mass, leave out the word *homily*, and make the preaching like something tacked on to the mass instead of part of it. So the situation is cool for the moment. But who knows what happens next."

"I still don't want this job," said the man. "It's corrupt. And I know I'm not clean to start with. But I can smell this."

"You have to keep something alive," said the bishop.

"Like what?"

"Those women's voices," said the bishop, "And a chance for those bigots."

"But they're hypocrites, the two, if they know what you're doing!"

"They don't know," said the bishop, "What they know is the truth, but they don't know what I know."

"Are you telling me I should have read Machiavelli instead of Matthew?"

"No, I'm telling you that the truth can destroy as much as a lie. And I'm telling you one more thing. You have to be the exception. You have to know the full truth and not be destroyed. And not destroy with it."

"This is Grand Inquisitor stuff," said the new man.

"No," said the bishop, "If I could get off this spot in the morning I would. This is no power. Every move I make does harm and good and I try to call it love, the service of love."

"That's because you're an icy stretch of road."

"You mean I'm slippery."

"Yes."

"Okay," said the bishop, "handle this straight. You've got a peace activist priest. And he's right on about these monster bombs we build. So he takes off two or three times a year to bases where he protests and gets hauled off to jail then let out on bail, which you put up. He's a terrific assistant when he's home. He also has a family. The mother and their two kids live up country. The guy's terrific counseling couples with marriage problems, and he's terrific with alcoholics, I don't know how. And you've just gotten the news of all this, as I have. You've gotten it from the parish, and the parish wants to keep him. And Rome will have your head if you do. Now what?"

"You suspend him with pay. You get him released from celibacy. You get him married so she's protected. And you hire him for Catholic Charities to work on social justice issues. Then you get Rome to reinstate him as a married priest and back he goes to the parish."

"And what about the woman priest?" said the bishop.

"She's a priest until Rome proves she's not."

"And the women preachers?"

"It's a special occasion every time. Therefore you can say okay."

"And the child molesters?"

"You let everybody know you have to obey the law."

"And the bigots?"

"You tell them charity covers a multitude of sins."

"Okay," said the bishop, "your way is right. But once you solve these problems you'll never hear another one as long as you're in office. Messy people don't come near clean ones. That's out of some old novel, *Country Priest* or something. But it's a fact. Now I'll follow your advice, if you will take this job. I'll make these clean decisions. But I want *you* to behave like a bleeding heart. People won't come to me, they'll come to you. And you'll be the real bishop. Agreed? Then we work out solutions so the law is kept, but it looks like you softened it. Agreed?"

The man sat there for a long time. "No," he said, "You be soft. I'm not there yet. I'll take the job if we can have it out like this all the time."

"Agreed," said the bishop. "Now something's come up. There's a priest who is going to run for Congress on a pro-life platform. To make pro-life the law of the land. He has publicly demanded my permission. I'm going to give it. And make a public statement that I myself never vote single issues."

21. Something for Nothing

For Ash Wednesday

We come therefore as Christ's ambassadors. It is as if God were appealing to you through us: in Christ's name, we implore you, be reconciled to God!

2 CORINTHIANS 5:20

A man stood in front of an art shop window in Kyoto one day. He was a foreigner in what was once a holy city. Something on display had stopped him. It was a Zen painting of a moon, a sheer mountain, and a pilgrim monk at the bottom washing his pilgrim feet in a clear stream. The sky was blue, the mountain black, with blacker pine trees clinging to the rocks, the monk was brown, and the water blue, as was the sky. The man loved the silk painting, so he went into the shop and purchased it. The seller rolled it as a scroll and gave it to the man, who put it under his arm and left the shop. He was filled with the beauty of what he had bought.

He stopped for a moment on the sidewalk to think what could he possibly do for the rest of that day. Then he saw a Buddhist monk seated on a low wall across the street. The monk rose and came to stand a few feet from the man and bowed to him and raised his hand palm upward toward the painting under the man's arm. Then he lowered his hand and stood there in peace and repose. The man knew the monk was asking for the painting. He did not respond for a long while, thinking all the thoughts he had to and staying still as the monk. Finally he took the scroll from under his arm and reached it toward the monk. But the monk raised his hand, palm toward the man as if in a sign of refusal. The man was puzzled. The monk turned and began to walk off in a way that asked the man to follow him. So the man did, and put the scroll back under his arm. The two came to the edge of a temple precinct not far from the shop. The monk paused at the lintel until the man came up. They removed their shoes and the monk gave the man the sleeve of his saffron robe to hold, and the man knew that this was a ritual of respect for him and for the sacred place. So he held the sleeve lightly in one hand and the scroll in the other as the monk led him through impoverished gardens and buildings until they came to a pagoda shrine that was empty of everything.

The monk led the man inside and there, on a blank wall, was a space lighter than the rest of the wall, as long and as narrow as the painting in the man's hand. And the man knew that the monk had sold his painting to stay alive. But he had not stayed alive, really. So the man walked away from the monk toward the wall, unrolled the painting and hung it where it had been. He went back beside the monk and looked and saw the moon, the mountain, and a monk washing his feet in the clear stream. It was as if the scene came out of nothing into something. The bare wall was nothing. The beauty of the scroll was everything. So he turned to the monk and bowed, took his sleeve and waited to be led outside. But the monk led him first toward a pool to the left of the shrine. It was circular, dark, and alive with large goldfish swimming slowly. Up in the sky was a day moon scarcely visible.

The monk placed the man near the edge of the pool so the day moon was over his head. Then the monk sat at the edge of the pool and washed his feet. And the man standing behind him knew the monk had made him the painting he had bought. After a time the monk rose and led the man to the street, where he left him. And the man stayed there for a long time thinking what could he possibly do for the rest of that day.

22. The Smell of Truth

For the First Sunday of Lent

Jesus answered, "Scripture says, 'Man cannot live on bread alone'"
LUKE 4:4

There was a woman who loved oranges, sweet Seville oranges. She loved peeling them as much as eating them—the light spray from the pressure of her hands had a wonderful smell. It filled whatever place she was in. And stayed on her hands a long time. Often when she was typing up a story with a particularly bad smell to it she would cup her hands over her mouth and nose and just breathe the scent that still clung to them. She had an Orange Bowl poster on the door of her cubicle, faces, footballs, leaping cheerleaders spraying out of an orange cut in half so its ribs showed and its flesh oozed life.

But nothing could overcome the smell of one particular story she had tracked down. She was a political reporter. Her husband was a lawyer. She had found out he was being blackmailed. He had once sold secrets to a foreign government when he was a young officer in the military. It was a friendly government, and he had done it to get some money so he could resign, go to law school, and have a career he could control a little better, which he had done. Then he had gotten involved in political consultation, and intergovernmental relations. It was very lucrative. He had kept to the ethics of his second profession. But he had told her none of this. And now he was being blackmailed into channeling funds from overseas into political campaigns at home, to candidates who were hawks against communism and who promoted the sale of arms to anticommunist groups around the world through overseas intermediaries. To intermediaries who happened to belong to the ministry of the friendly government he had sold secrets to many years before. A very, very lucrative business. And he was doing it to protect his career. His whole life. He felt that his earlier misbehavior had been minimal. Exposure meant trial for treason. Her life and the lives of their two children now in college would be ruined. If he ever got to trial—they could kill him first.

They could also kill her if she handed in the story she was now typing up and it appeared tomorrow in the early edition. It would have been impossible for anyone but her to have found out. She knew he was neither hawk nor dove. But a year or so back he began to associate with hawkish candidates in ways he laughed off, saying his involvement was purely professional. She smelled fear in him, the way she smelled oranges even across an open space. She also felt him saying, "Leave me be. This is something you cannot know." She even felt him saying, "If you know, I'm dead." He was conscious of none of this, but he was desperate to conceal his past and his present. And some of his trips departed from every pattern.

Someone must have detected her suspicion, someone watching her, or he had told someone. Because then there came a tip, by note, which led her down certain trails, through certain political figures, to the funds her husband was leaving with campaign managers, funds that seemed to come to him from nowhere and to which he gave legitimate names, monies too small to attract attention but frequent enough to pile up into large sums. She was being led to know. So as to be kept quiet. And the second tip led her not to funds but to newspaper accounts of a good many years back about the leak of secrets to friendly foreign governments and the inability of the military to track down the sources of the leaks. Someone had given her a two and a two. She knew the four for herself.

She typed in the last bit of the scenario and sat back in her chair to decide whether to clip the sheets and put them on the editor's desk, complete with references to back the story. Or to tear the copy to shreds now that she had put the whole story together and knew what she would destroy. She reached over to her coat hanging on the rack, pulled an orange out of the pocket, and almost abstractedly broke into it with her thumb. She peeled it slowly, in chunks like continents, and laid them like petals in the ashtray she used for them, never for cigarettes. Then she noticed she was building a flower, the larger peels below, the smaller above, the navel for the flower bud. "This delicious life can go on," she thought. "Or it can stop with a last bite and maybe no good come from the destruction of a few careers. Because the candidates could say they didn't know. And the campaign managers could say they were careless in the heat of things and trusted the donors to be on the up and up. Negligence, not malice. And those members of that foreign ministry could deny complicity to the hilt, or plead an imprudent kind of patriotism." And she thought her husband might even win compassion from a civil court and not get a treason charge, though he would get hit, and hard. If he survived.

The sweet orange was bitter in her mouth, and in that instant she knew who really had to pay the price. Her love had to become like a hatred if she broke her silence and published the story. Love of husband becomes hatred of husband, love of children becomes hatred of children, love of self becomes hatred of self, everything pulled inside out and for what? The way you lay open the wedges of an orange. She saw the light flashing on her phone, and she looked through the glass partition to the secretary who simply mouthed the words, "Your husband."

She raised ten fingers to the secretary, shook her head, and saw the secretary tell him to call back in ten minutes. In less than a minute the light flashed again, and she looked through the glass. The secretary shrugged her shoulders, meaning someone who refused to identify him or herself, as those who tip off things usually do. She shook her head no and the light stopped.

But another flashed instantly, and this time the secretary came to the door and said, "High level, ambassadorial, heavy accent."

"No," the woman said, "And no one for a while, please." In the next few minutes she had a vision of what silence was. The orange peels in the ashtray were not flower petals anymore, and the navel not a flower bud. They were debris. Debris of camps, of causes, of conspiracies. Life torn apart for someone's sweet tooth. It was

then she loved oranges for their voice. "Silence is the last temptation," she thought. "I can have the whole thing if I keep my mouth
shut. I can have nothing if I open it."

She took the story sheets, clipped them together, and walked
the length of the cubicle corridor and put the story on her distracted editor's desk. She knew in a short while he would not be
distracted. Her work had never proven to be wrong. And the
morning paper would be explosive. She walked back to her cubicle and sat waiting for her husband's call. She looked at the
orange peels and said, "What do I make of you now?"

His phone call came in, and he said, "Have you told anyone?"
in a voice so controlled she knew he was desperate to know if the
blackmail on her had worked. If she said "No," she could keep
him alive for a short while. There was someone else listening on
that phone. "Yes" might mean she would never see him again.
"No" might mean she would never get across the street to hail a
cab. Then again, "Yes" might mean someone would call and ask
her how her children were and name the exact houses they lived
in at their separate colleges—as if to ask, "Do you want to see them
again?"

She saw her editor standing outside the glass with "Fantastic!"
written all over his face and yet looking as if he knew her life
would come down around her head.

"It will be in the morning paper," she said to her husband. "And
put no one else on this line, the voices are being recorded. I have
named names, so if those who are listening want to risk murder
charges too, let them go ahead. I can also write obituaries." The
line was silent. Then he put the phone down. She looked through
the glass to her editor, waved him quietly to go ahead, then took
the orange peels up in her hands and wept into them until they
smelled of her, not she of them. The smell of debris.

23. Carnal Knowledge

For the Second Sunday in Lent

We, by contrast, are citizens of heaven, and from heaven we expect our
deliverer to come, the Lord Jesus Christ.

PHILIPPIANS 3:20

There was a man who worked for Graves Registration in the army.
He had done it for years. And had years to go before he retired.
He had seen the human body in every state of decay imaginable,
mainly men's bodies, but enough women and children to be an
expert at saying who they were from the very little left of them. He
was somewhat of an artist and so could draw from fragments
what people maybe looked like before whatever hit them did. It
was a skill particularly needed to help families identify air crash
victims pulled out of smoking wrecks.

He always knew when he had gotten it right when he stood
with someone over remains and showed them his reconstruction.
There was a kind of collapse of recognition. He would then put
the drawing back in a folder to go with the rest of the data on this
particular body. No one asked him for the drawing. And people
forgot he had ever made one. He was in too grisly a business. It
meant staring for as long as he could take it at someone's ruined
face, then allowing a power of imagination in him to go to work,
he never knew how, and gradually as he used his charcoal pencil
on white coarse-grained paper, a face would begin to emerge he
would feel right about. He even tried details, eyes open, hair
combed this or that way. Just enough to be a ghost of the dead self,
not enough to give the impression the person was not dead.

In recent years he noticed that this power of imagination was
beginning to work without him. It seemed to take charcoal and
paper all by itself and work on the living things that he met. It was
not hallucination, nor some attempt of his soul to save itself from
the grim business he had forced it to be in. In fact, it was a power

that kept him very realistic and very sane. There'd be an old dog just about able to pee, and stroke, stroke, the man would make a mental sketch of it looking up to a stick it was ready to jump for. Or there would be an old, toothless woman begging on the corner, and he would put her back in young flesh, then wonder what brought her to a corner to beg. All of this was strictly physical. There was nothing he could do about the hatreds, the cursings, the distortions of people in riots.

He found out by accident that he could do some good with his power to sketch the young by looking at the old. He was visiting a home for the elderly. He thought a distant relative was there, but she wasn't. So he got to talking to a very old woman who didn't make much sense. She thought he was a priest come to hear her confession, so she sat him down and started to tell him all her sins had come from being so beautiful when she was young. He asked her for a photo, and she rummaged in some papers, then gave up saying they were stored in a library somewhere. They were works of art.

He looked and found a paper placemat, took a heavy pencil from his pocket, and said, "Let me draw you when you were young."

She let him. She gained a kind of clarity as he drew, working from what she was to what she must have been. He made a lot of mistakes which he had to erase, but gradually he could see life come into her features as it came into the drawing. And then there was a moment when he recognized her from his own drawing before he could recognize her from her actual face. She had been one of the great strippers of the thirties when he had been a kid in parochial school. He and his pals had used a rainy day as an excuse to go see her, in a theater torn down long ago. He had needed a priest for that.

"My paper isn't big enough," he said to her. He went into the lobby and took a very large Sacred Heart calendar off the wall, quickly before anyone saw, and returned to the glassed-in porch where he had found her. She was looking at her face in the sketch with a kind of strange joy. He worked over her shoulder as he did a fine copy of it to scale on the white cardboard back of the calendar. Then he put under the chin the round shoulder he remembered, then the hint of a breast starting out, then a lovely hand holding a veil—that was a Salome dance, he recalled—then beautiful ribs, and swelling hips just concealed by another veil hanging down back, then long legs, like the ones in *Esquire* many years ago, high heels that were slippers, and there she was as she had been that rainy day. And he showed it to her. But she wasn't looking any more. It was her face she had recaptured and was pressing the place mat to her like the veil she had pressed many years ago. She was happy. And she was asleep.

"What do I do with this," he thought, "one side Sacred Heart, the other side stripper?" He left her, holding the stripper side against his own chest, the Sacred Heart out. He smiled at a couple of staff members. When they were not looking, he hung the calendar back on the wall, Sacred Heart outward. "They won't find it until next January," he thought, "and they probably won't know who she is."

From that time on he used to go visit hospitals that would permit it and ask old people to let him guess in a drawing what they looked like when they were young. He would look at no picture— he'd just have them talk him into getting it right. It was amazing to see people come up with several versions of the same self at the same age. Or be unable to and settle for something like a caricature. Or come up with a synthesis of their whole lives.

There was one week, though, when he couldn't go anywhere. A planeload of young men had not made it far off the ground. Some were unrecognizable, and he had spent a long time on the scene, along with other experts. When he finished, he went out to his favorite restaurant, a German place, and sat down for the familiar ritual of his meal. He loved the old mahogany bar across from the crowded tables, and the sign over it, *suum cuique*, "to each his own." He ordered some wurst, sauerkraut, and dark beer, with dark bread and a bowl of butter. And then he waited. And as he waited, faces began to form in his mind. And this time he knew his soul was hurting and trying to defend itself against the grisly job he had just had to do. So he let it. The faces seemed

to come from paintings he knew rather than corpses he had iden-
tified, but they were the same faces. They were a soft rose color,
very alive, very warm, filled with love of something, drifting
towards him like masks, but living masks, then receding into the
background without seeming to lose their existence, as if they
were just showing him they were alive someplace. "All right," he
said, "all right." And the faces quietly disappeared.

The waiter plunked down the large beer, the bread and butter
and said, "Plate in a minute."

The man liked the gruffness of the place, the sawdust on the
floor, and the civility. But he couldn't lift his hand to take the beer.
There was a joy in him that had him immobilized.

"All right," he said, "all right." And the joy quietly disappeared.
He waited for a sadness to come but none did. Then he picked up
the beer and took a sip of its thick, musty liquid, just as the waiter
put down the plate in front of him, steaming wurst and sauerkraut, plus a pot of good sharp mustard. "Good eating, but where
are the strippers?" the man asked his soul, half aloud.

"You got the wrong place for that, buddy!" said the waiter. "A
ton of them around the corner. Eat first. Look later." And he left.

"They go with the faces," the man said. Then he was sad. But
only until he tasted the mustard.

24. Skeletons

For the Third Sunday of Lent

But he replied, "Leave it, sir, this one year while I dig round it and
manure it. And if it bears next season, well and good; if not, you shall
have it down."

LUKE 13:8–9

There was a man who loved old books. It was his career to handle
them for buyers and sellers. He had become an expert in one kind

from the early 1500s, books dealing with the vanity of human life, ones that had marvelous woodcuts of skeletons. There were skeletons dancing in a ring, skeletons marrying one another, a bony hand putting a ring on a bony finger. There were birth skeletons, a small cage of bones coming out of a larger cage of bones into a skeletal midwife's hands. And she was smiling.

In that world everyone smiled. There were no frowning skeletons. And that was what fascinated the man. It was a world of all virtue and no vice. There was time, fleshless time, striding through a harvest festival with a great scythe over his shoulder and a few tatters of clothing streaming in the wind he himself was making. There was the Pope signing a condemnation, while a skeleton behind him placed a skull cap on his own head. And there was the Grand Inquisitor looking up from his soup to see a skeleton holding a steaming tureen full of shattered ribs.

The skeletons were not devils. They seemed to want to chase people to heaven rather than to hell, to keep them from harm, like skull and crossbone signs on high tension wire pylons. Needless to say, these books were not the world's favorites. And almost no one read the texts, discourses filled with violent language against the vanities of life, filled with wise counsel on how to be dead to life so as to live after death. But not as a skeleton. That was the paradox. Life after death for the virtuous would be harmonious and fleshly, like music from St. Cecilia's harmonium. Life after death for the vicious would not be skeletal, it would be fleshly and chaotic, scenes from Dante's Hell.

The man had his office walls decorated with enlargements of the woodcuts he found most interesting—the one of the leap-frogging skeletons, for example, or the one of the galloping skeletal horse with skeletal rider leaping over a fence of bayonets with absolute immunity. There were the three graces, Joy, Bloom, Brilliance, as skeletons dancing in a ring. Then a discus-throwing skeleton. Then a Venus skeleton with one hand across to hide her breasts and one hand down to hide her crotch, and a smile at the one who looked at her for the irony of having neither. This one was right over the back of the man's chair.

One day a young woman came in with a very old book to sell. It was one he recognized. At the very same moment he knew it was stolen, but not by the young woman. The thief would have known the book and would have noticed that just over the back of his chair was the Venus woodcut from that very book. But the woman wasn't looking at any of the blow-ups on the wall. Maybe she was fencing it for someone—it was worth about $20,000 the last time he had handled its sale. So he went right for the truth.

"This is a stolen book," he said. "Who sent you to me?"

"It's my father's book," she said. "The old bastard finally died. Gave almost everything away to the Boy Scouts. Left me the house and the junk in it. This is part of the junk. My boyfriend said it's worth something. We looked you up in the Yellow Pages."

"What's your father's name?" the man said.

She told him a name.

"I don't recognize him," he said. "I have on file the name of the last person who bought it. My guess is if I check recent thefts I'll find my former customer has been robbed. I'm supposed to report stolen property."

"Then report it," she said. "But I didn't steal it. It was in his house. He did screwy things with his money. That's a stupid book."

"All right, I'll report it," he said. "I don't know your name, but there'll be an alarm out for the book, if you should try to sell it elsewhere. And I know what you look like."

The woman was silent. "You might as well keep it," she said. "That's what you want, isn't it? A little black-mail? So you can play hero? Make a little dough yourself?"

"The book's important to me," he said.

"Important, shit! I took a quick look. It's for creeps. Like you!"

"Here, just take it," he said. "Just open it gently. Open it to page 57."

The woman did so. She was agitated, trying to figure how to get out of this situation.

"Now look up over my head at the blown-up photo."

"Astrology," the woman said. "Venus. I'm not Venus, I'm Pisces."

"It's not astrology. It's *memento mori.*"

"And what's that?"

"It means that someday soon you won't have any breasts or any crotch. And you won't have any boyfriend to use them with."

"What do you mean?" she said.

"I mean you'll be behind bars for a few years. And if you make fencing a career, you'll be behind bars a lot of years."

"You're a cruel bastard," she said as she put the book back on his desk. "Here, keep it, sleep with it. Make a lot of noise trying to screw. Like garbage trucks."

"I don't want to keep it," he said. "I want you to keep it. In your pocket where it'll fit. So you can keep screwing. And not like a garbage truck either. Like somebody's who's not ripping somebody off."

"And you make sure I can't sell it?" she said.

"Correct," he said. "But I can't make sure you don't pitch it in a fire someplace. I want to keep that book alive."

"You must love death. Look at these walls!"

"They're not dead. They're having a hell of a time at our expense. Pardon the pun. They're naked and nobody gets turned on. They're smiling and nobody laughs. They're playing and nobody wants to play. And you can't kill them but nobody wants to be unkillable that way."

"So what am I supposed to do?" she asked, "Let you have it?"

"No, oh no," he said. "We do this. I take an envelope especially for books. I write the address of the man who owns this book on it. I use your pen and I write left-handed instead of my normal right. I put enough stamps on it, seal it, give it to you. Then I stand here at the window, right next to Joy, Bloom, and Brilliance, the three skeleton graces, and I watch the mail box across the street. And I watch you out of the building, across the street, put the package in the mail box. You don't have to. You can keep it. I report it. But you drop it in the box and we have a secret between us."

"What do you get out of that?" she said. "Wouldn't you like to see me a skeleton behind bars?"

"Oh no," he said. "Look over my head again. At that Venus. She's much better with breasts and crotch. That's what these skeletons do. They tell you what's much better."

"Write the address," the woman said.

So the man did. And sealed the book in the envelope, then handed it to her.

"What do I tell my boyfriend?" she said.

"Don't tell him anything," the man said.

"What do you mean?" she said.

"You get rid of him too," the man said.

25. Really No Choice

For the Fourth Sunday of Lent

From first to last this has been the work of God. He has reconciled us men to himself through Christ, and he has enlisted us in this service of reconciliation.

2 CORINTHIANS 5:18

There was a woman, an only child, who took care of her sick mother until her mother died. The daughter was a nurse, so she was deft at taking care of the sick and didn't flap easily. And the two got along very well, for the long time that the mother was ill. The father had disappeared years ago for some reason, and the two had lost track of him. The daughter had no interest in him. Within a few days of the burial the daughter found that her mother had left her nothing in her will, and there had been a substantial amount, in savings and in property, including the house they lived in, though the daughter was not sure where it had all come from. She got nothing, not even the house. It all went to a name she did not recognize. The will dated way back, to a time when no one could doubt her mother's mind. And it had been reaffirmed frequently right up to recent years. The daughter felt absolute betrayal, not fury, not frenzy, but as if there were no weight left to things. They could drift any way they wanted.

"Who is this person?" she said to her mother's lawyer.

"She's your half-sister," said the lawyer.

"No such thing," said the woman.

"Yes," said the lawyer. "I'll let you guess or I'll explain."

"A natural child?"

"Yes," said the lawyer.

Suddenly the world seemed to have weight again, too much weight.

"Where is she?" said the woman. She knew there had to be more strange details.

"I'll have to show you," said the lawyer. "And one more thing. The will stipulates that I am to remain the administrator of her estate. You will soon see why."

He took her in a cab across town to a main shopping street. They got out, and he said to her, "We have to walk this street. She'll be somewhere along it."

So they walked for maybe fifteen minutes. Then he stopped her and said, "Now look, on that subway grate."

So she did, and saw a derelict woman surrounded by her things in several plastic bags. She was sitting with her knees drawn up, asleep, shapeless in clothes, but her hand was out, and some coins were sliding off her palm down through her fingers.

"I'm supposed to take care of her for the rest of my life, or hers," the lawyer said.

"How do you do that? She'll be stolen blind or killed for all the money she'll now have."

"She won't know," said the lawyer. "She won't know why the cops pick her up on this or that night. Or why an ambulance stops for her, thinking she's someone else. Or why nobody beats her up. Or why someone sneaks a needle into her, and it's not drugs. Or who bails her out when she does some stealing. She doesn't know where the sweaters come from, or who makes sure she's not out on a night she'll freeze. It costs. It costs a lot."

The woman looked again and said, "You're sure it's she?"

"Yes," the lawyer said, "even to the finger prints."

"And there's no reaching her?" the woman asked.

"No. We spent years trying. Her mind is gone."

"If she were to die right now where would that money go?"

The lawyer moved uneasily.

"I have no intention of harming her," said the woman, "not for any amount of money."

"The money would go to a hostel for such people as she," the lawyer answered.

"My bet is I can break that will," the woman said.

"You'd bet correctly, a good part of it anyway," he answered.

"Would she be less protected?"

"Yes. Someone might not check her on a freezing night."

"Well, mother," the woman said, "you're not the only one who is paying." Then she moved the ten yards and reached down to turn her sister's head slightly so she could see her features, the vein-ridden cheek, the runny nose, the tooth that showed. Even at a short distance the woman had smelled the alcohol and the urine. She walked back to the lawyer.

"Get someone to take her in and clean her up," she said.

"Someone will, soon," he said. "I keep tabs."

"Then it's hers," the woman said, "the money. And she's mother's. And they won't be long apart."

"I'll have to sell the house," said the lawyer. "I could sell it to you."

"No, no, I'll leave it. I have my savings, I have my profession, and I have some life left. I must decide what to do with that."

The two of them stood there looking at her sister on the grate.

"I'll walk the rest of the street, then walk back to her here, and I'll know by that time what to do," she said.

"Let me wait for you," said the lawyer.

"You don't have to," she said.

"True," he said, "but you would do me a favor to let me."

"Okay." And she began her walk from the point where her sister sat. She saw that her mother could love recklessly. So could whoever the man was. And her mother could love badly. As her father could. And she saw that her mother could love well, and maybe her father could too, somewhere. And she saw that her sister could now do neither. But that others could, for money, do the right thing by her, however minimal it was to haul her in on a bad night. And she saw that her mother took advantage of love, right to the last minute. Because it was the only way she could try to help what she had harmed.

"And what about me, mother?" she said as she turned. She was now walking away from the sun on that east/west street. It was low. And as she approached people she saw that the color of sunset was on their faces, rosy, pink. And they were not aware of it. As she had not been when walking in their direction.

"I will not make a life of bitterness," she said. "I will make a life of beauty, cost what it may. And I will do it with my body, with my hands. And it will be with patients who do not know what hit them, with children."

She was back at the subway grate, but her sister was gone, and she knew where. The lawyer was nearby watching her. She walked to him and looked at him with great calm.

"She was yours too, wasn't she?" she said.

He said nothing. He waited, then said, "Have you decided what to do?"

"For others, yes," she said. "For myself, no. I can't do that. It has to come the way the color comes on people's faces, like this evening, in this sunset."

"I need you to understand," he said.

"I will," she said, "but at the moment I need to keep walking. When the sun is gone, I'll come by. And you can talk."

26. Sticks and Stones

For the Fifth Sunday of Lent

Here am I, a witness in my own cause, and my other witness is the Father who sent me." They asked, "Where is your father?" Jesus replied, "You know neither me nor my Father; if you knew me you would know my Father as well."

JOHN 8:7–8

A man and a woman were having drinks in the Erin-Go-Pub on St. Patrick's Day night. He was drinking Guinness Stout and she Perrier water.

"Marvelous," he said, "right out of the peat bog!"

"There's rust," she said, "all over your mouth, it's corroding you already."

"What a way to die!" he said. "Beats being stoned."

"You mean drugs?" she asked.

"What else could I mean?" he replied, then added, "Your face has gone all pale. What's in that water besides Mother Nature from the center of the earth?"

"I just got a flash recall of that Sunday gospel," she said, "You know, the one where they were going to stone that woman for adultery. It's been in my head all week!"

"Listen, you know philosophy, the rocks are not in your head, it's the image of the rocks!"

"The rust of that Stout has gone to your brain. I'm serious. I feel brutalized by that scene."

"Now don't disrespect this Stout," he said, "It goes flat if you do and flat Stout can harm your soul."

"You're not helping me," she said. "And I'm going to ruin your evening if I don't get this image of that gospel out of my head."

"Well, Jesus stopped them," the man said. "No rocks flew that day. She walked away with a scare and that's it. Listen, they're playing the 'Rakes of Mallow.'"

"Sounds like everything else they play," she said. "What if the scribes hadn't listened? Have you seen the rocks they use in the Middle East?"

"Oh, come on now," he said, "something else is going on. There are rocks all over the world and people throw them. That Scripture reading really hurt you for some other reason."

"Well, I feel so vulnerable."

And he said, "There isn't a rock within a mile of this pub unless it's in a drink. Listen, it's 'Danny Boy,' and the tenor is gargling it beautifully."

She said, "How did Jesus ever stop them? How does anyone ever stop them? Is it just when you're smart? Or you're God and they get a whiff of your power? You certainly don't if you're a woman!"

"Oh, that's it," he said, "You want to be the one to stop the stoners of this world and you think you can't."

And she said, "All I can do is make your beer flat. Look, the foam is gone and it's sagging in the middle like coffee grounds."

"I'll bite it as I drink it and that will liven it up."

She said, "I cannot stop the stoners. You are right. That's what has gotten to me. I think of Holden Caulfield in *The Catcher In The Rye* wanting to go all over the world wiping out the 'F-you's' so his little sister Phoebe wouldn't be harmed in her soul. Well, names will never hurt Phoebe. The sticks and stones will. Now you look glum," she said. "I'm ruining your Paddy's Day night!"

"Never, never! If I had a solution to anything it'd be you."

"What if Jesus heard you say that?"

"He'd love it. Look, I think he'd have gotten between those stones and those throwers and that woman."

"Because he was the Savior?"

"No, you know better than that."

"Because he loved her?"

"He didn't even know who she was," the man said.

"Then why?"

"The same reason as you," the man said. "He felt how vulnerable this one woman was. He felt how vulnerable he was. If she died, he died, and he knew it."

"Yes," she said, "if that woman died, then Jesus died. That's John Donne's poem, isn't it? 'Seek not to know for whom the bell tolls, it tolls for thee!'"

"Well," the man said, "it's more than that. It's you sitting here with all those rocks in your head, and I love you for it better than I love this Guinness Stout. And Jesus had rocks in his head too. That's why you're so alike. And if any harm ever came to you, I'd die."

"They're playing 'Brennan On The Moor,'" she said. "Everyone's blood will be boiling in two minutes. I don't want your blood ever to boil."

"Not even for you?" he said.

"Well, maybe," she said, "when they play 'Kathleen Mavourneen.'"

"Oh, they will," he said. "Then watch this beer go flat!"

27. The Christa Crucifix

For Passion Sunday

> Yet he did not think to snatch at equality with God, but made himself nothing, assuming the nature of a slave. Bearing the human likeness, revealed in human shape, he humbled himself, and in obedience accepted even death—death on a cross.
>
> PHILIPPIANS 1:7–8

There was a priest who saw a notice in the paper about a Christa crucifix being put on display in a theological school library. Christ was a naked woman nailed to a cross. But the photo in the paper was too blurry for the priest to see much, though what he did see infuriated him. And kept infuriating him during the successive weeks until one day, a day off from the parish, he got in his old clothes and went to see this thing.

There was just the receptionist at the library, he was the only one going in to look, so he asked where, and she pointed to behind some moveable room dividers with artistic posters pinned to them, Virgins of Vladimir, Czestochowa, Chartres, and Montserrat. Set up to form a Z, the room dividers were an indication of what the viewer was to see.

"It's like a fun house," the priest snapped to himself. "You can get in, but not out." He rounded the corners and came into the larger room, stopped, and said to himself, "Where is it?" He was expecting something lifesize.

Then he spotted it, to his right, and it was very small, maybe a foot and a half high, and it was done in rosewood that had been stained darker to give it a look of being bloody. The body on it was absolutely exquisite, despite the blood smears, the nail and spear holes, and the clotted hair with the crown of thorns binding it in like a jogger's headband. And it was absolutely naked, no breechclout, as there would have been on a Christus. The breasts, the hips, the crotch, the knees were almost twitching with pain, they looked so alive. And the face was still living and trying to draw breath.

"Well, I'll be damned," the priest said. "This is more suffering than I've ever seen on anyone before. And I've never seen such a beautiful body. Somebody is fooling with me."

He turned and walked toward the windows at the other end of the library room, a Gothic room with some pitiful stained glass lancets of circuit rider preachers in the green hills. Then he turned and walked with slow liturgical steps back toward the crucifix to see what his real reaction would be. And once again he was struck by the suffering loveliness of the figure, the astonishing physical maturity, the straining outward of its whole being toward someone's arms—yes, arms!

"Damn," he said again, "what's happening to me? This just won't fly. It's too erotic. That woman comes right through those wounds. There'd be filthy talk about it. We'd really get it from the other religions. If they didn't smash this thing, they'd wrap it in bandages and call it a mummy."

The priest actually kicked himself. Because he saw what he was doing. He was using ridicule to defend himself against this. He had called it a thing. It wasn't. It was a she. And whatever he had said at first about the beauty, he now could see the horror. And a different kind of anger came over him.

"You can't do this to that form, you can't do this to a woman. Not for anybody's good." But he knew that was another dodge. Women had been ravaged worse than this, and from the start.

"But it's not Christ," he said to himself. "I'm getting a lesson in something else."

He stood looking at it until his feelings had settled back to the sense of beauty and horror he had felt first. And after a while he realized that he loved that form, because it was itself and not Christ or anyone else, but it was straining outward toward everyone it could see. As if its suffering was just beginning.

"Oh damn," the priest said at that thought. "That's what it brings me to do, make sense of myself."

He noticed then that there was a guest book on a stand some feet to the side of the statue.

"Not for a funeral, I hope," he said as he walked over to it and looked at its open pages. It was a book of comments. There were some already. Some glorious trash about women being the God beyond God, some inglorious trash about nakedness and blasphemy. Some theological jargon the priest actually giggled at as he remembered the dry, dusty classrooms the jargon came from, and the sexless monsters they all were at the time, writing the words down to memorize because careers were at stake.

So he took up the pen and wrote, "It's perfect. Keep it on display. But keep it here."

By now a few other people were in the room, a young couple, an old man, maybe an emeritus professor holding a very precious book in one hand, a cane in the other.

The young man said, "Oh wow, she looks like she's doing it for somebody's kicks."

"Ugh," said the young woman. "I mean you, ugh," and she gave him a loving shove on the arm.

The old man muttered something about "Stupid" and went to

have a closer look. The priest felt wounded and said to himself, "I'd better go."

As he went by the receptionist's desk she looked up and said, "Did you like it?"

He stopped and said very firmly, but softly, "Yes," and then paused because he realized she hoped for more. So he simply said the word again, very firmly, very softly, "Yes." And he left.

It wasn't a minute before he felt infuriated again, as if he had just been subjected to a spell. So he stopped right there in the street to give himself a lesson.

"You're not easy to fool, right?"

"Right."

"You weren't fooled by that Christa, right?"

"Right."

"That's just a woman, not a god, right?"

"Right."

"So she's no threat to Jesus, right?"

"Right."

"So you can go home and forget about her, right?"

"Wrong."

"Okay, so you can go home and keep your mouth shut about her, right?"

"Wrong."

"Okay, so you can go home and live with this thing like it's your own soul, right?"

"Right."

"So you don't have to be angry at her anymore, right?"

"Right."

The priest felt a tug at his arm. It was a bag lady looking for money.

"Right," he said and gave her the coins in his pocket.

A young woman gave him a smile that could have meant, "You're fine," or "You're real dumb."

"Right," he said. "Go home. They'll get to you like this."

But it was too late. A dog looking for affection came off the muddy grass and jumped up on him to get him in the game.

28. My God, How Simple!

For Easter Sunday

> Your self-satisfaction ill becomes you. Have you never heard the saying,
> "A little leaven leavens all the dough?"
>
> 1 CORINTHIANS 5:6

A woman was looking for the perfect monastery. To live in as a contemplative. Not to visit as a tourist. When she was alone with God there was nothing like it. It was a peace and a love which consumed her life. But something always seemed to happen. She would grow aware of deep divisions among the sisters. In one group the division was inside/outside, part of them wanting to turn the place into a shelter for the homeless, the other part wanting to lock the door to the street, throw away the key, and live off the oranges that grew in the orchard. Her sense of love and peace disappeared, until a day came when she knew she had to leave or turn into something like the dry well in the cloister garden.

So she joined a teaching order that kept a school inside its walls, for pre-college girls. It was an order that insisted on a great deal of prayer outside school hours. And that proved to be a different, insoluble problem. The girls loved her and ate her up. She was caught in corridors, in the library, even in the evenings over the phone, and she listened to them thrashing happily or sadly through the great sexual revolution of their lives. She had little energy for anything else, and a deep pain of loss inside her. She loved those girls too, not for the adulation they gave her, but for the joy they were bursting with and for their pain. She saw tragedies in the making and tragedies already made. There were drugs in the lavatory, and sex on the hockey field, and plain old lying that was affixed to some tongues like a tattoo to a sailor's arm.

"There must be a place for me," she thought. So she left the teaching group.

Now she was on a train going up into the mountains to a monastery she had known about for a long time.

"If this fails," she thought, "I'll go back to teaching. And whoever it is I miss will have to miss me."

To her right, out the window, narrow gorges appeared, and the train began to pass through short tunnels. The shapes of the earth were marvelous, very steep, like gorges in Chinese paintings, trees growing straight up, out of rock faces going straight down. And water rushing. And shadow and light and the effects of clouds. Frequent stops at small villages, a few people getting on, a few off. Finally the train levelled out, running along the edge of a plateau. "If this train would just keep climbing," she thought. And it could, there were mountains further off to the right, not far away.

She had been alone in the eight-person compartment for most of the trip. At a stop near the foot of one of the more spectacular peaks, a man came into the compartment, stowed his gear in the rack, and sat down with a deep breath of satisfaction. He had climbers' stuff on, the boots, the knickers and knee socks, the sweaters, the windbreaker, the watch cap. And he was in his sixties so he was down to a lean face red from the wind, bearded gray, and quiet. But very sharp blue eyes that quickly took her in, not aggressively, but the way someone does who is used to wide scenes of great beauty. He reached in a pocket for a granola bar, unwrapped it, broke half of it off and offered it to her. She hesitated, thinking he needed the energy more than she did. He recognized that, and simply nodded to her to take it if she wished. So she did. It was the kind that had good molasses in it, and she knew she'd have to poke some free of her teeth with her finger. She mimicked chewing on tar to the man, and he put his head back and laughed without a sound.

The train was rolling again. It would travel a few hours more at this pace. The man finished his granola bar and very carefully put the wrapper back in his windbreaker pocket. Then he stretched his legs out and leaned his head into the angle of the headrest and within a few minutes was asleep.

"O, thank God," the woman thought. "If he ever snored!"

He was amazingly composed. She looked at him without prying, much as he had looked at her. The gray, close-cut hair, the gray, well-trimmed beard, the flush from the wind still on his face. And his hands crossed in front of him, no ring, hard hands, but not from work, from climbing maybe. She turned back to the scenery. The train had curved away from the last stop and she could see the mountain he had been on, not much in itself, but it looked out on marvelous views.

About a half hour later the man woke up, yawned again without a sound, sat up straight, then reached in his other pocket and took out a marvelous fat orange. He peeled it and filled the compartment with a beautiful light scent. Then he broke it into some wedges and offered her a few wedges, anticipating her refusal by a double nod of his head. So she took them and was grateful for the very sweet taste, and for the sense of sharing the man seemed to have. He ate what he had with his eyes closed, it was so good. When he had finished, he looked at her with this terrific smile to say, "Wasn't it delicious?"

Then his eyes moved past her to the scenery. He saw it receding; she saw it advancing. When the train crossed to the other wide of a gorge their heads turned, and she could see him, as he could certainly see her, responding to the beauty of the scenery. After a while, she opened her hands palm up on her lap to tell him she had nothing to offer but wished she had. He just lifted his hands up, palms together in a prayer sign, Indian fashion; then, as if thinking something further, he swung his hands slightly toward the scene outside the train window, dropped them again, and went back inside himself in a way she recognized.

"He has known the love and peace," she thought. "But he knows how to share it and I don't. A granola bar, an orange, my God, how simple!"

She felt a tremendous shift begin inside her. Like a shift of the earth that had produced some of these mountains.

"He will come to me," she thought. "What am I chasing him for? The peace and the love are mine. Granola bar and orange, my

God, how simple. Except I have neither. But if I had said no, this would have been an awful compartment, and an awful trip."

The train began to slow, so she stood up, got her suitcase, and put on her coat against the fresh wind outside. The man had a mountain flower in what looked like a tee holder sewn to his windbreaker. He took it, held it for a moment to his nose, nodded that it still had its scent, then reached it toward her. She took it and caught its scent also, light but clear, and she put it in the lapel of her coat. As she got to the door she put out her hand, and he took it. Then she descended from the train and went to the ticket window in the waiting room of the station.

She bought a return ticket and asked when the next train would go back down to the city.

"Two hours from now," the man said.

She looked for a place to buy granola bars and oranges but there was none. So she bought some chocolate.

"Put it in your outside pocket," she said to herself, thinking of the blouses she had had to wash.

"Now we'll see what comes," she said as she waited for the train to take her back.

29. The Power of Fragile Things

For the Second Sunday of Easter

Jesus said, "Because you have seen me you have found faith. Happy are they who never saw me and yet have found faith."

JOHN 20:29

There was a man who became a cynic against his own wishes. It happened underneath his wishes. And he was amused, the way one is amused at seeing a horse urinate on a city street, people skipping free of the splash and looking at the mounted cop as if he has pushed a button. But the man was also frightened.

Because it created a vacuum in his life, and he found the vacuum more and more comfortable.

He observed the normal rituals: love to his wife, attention to his children, carefulness with his work. He was an auditor for the federal government, so he saw a lot of figures on a lot of things, from brass bedposts to varieties of nose cones. He knew them from their numbers. After a while, in fact, there was a certain joy to the vacuum which was only upset when he tried to believe something, thinking that believe he must or he'd end up immoral or a terror. He'd listen to the Pope or the Dalai Lama or the Ayatollah, and his vacuum would begin to writhe. Like the flocks of birds he used to see at sunset far off, turning, twisting, like appearing and disappearing cyclones. The birds were warming themselves against the long cold night by their crazy swings through the sky. They also flew that way in the morning to shake off the cold of the night. That's what this vacuum was doing, shaking things off.

Propaganda, the propaganda of the woman on the bench along the street who whimpered about how bad things were as she held her hand out. And who looked at the money he gave her with an eager eye even as she kept whimpering.

"I'm not a cynic," he thought. "I'm a disbeliever, I'm like the bubble in a carpenter's rule."

His wife had noticed all this. But she never pried. Though he began to notice certain changes in her behavior, as if she were inviting him to say something. They had never had a bowl of flowers on the breakfast table, even though she loved flowers. Usually they just had some interesting placemats from spots where they had vacationed. Washable ones, because the children ate as if from troughs in their hurry to get away to something more interesting. But now there were often flowers on the table. And the flowers were always very small, very delicate, baby's breath, or primroses, beside a single fern. The flowers touched him like a pleasure, he knew, but never stayed in his vacuum long enough to reveal their kinship.

One night he noticed a change in the bed sheets. They were new sheets with a very light pattern of irises on ivory cotton. In fact his cheek rested on one while she sat reading and the light showed he was in a basket of them. But he said nothing, just fell into a sound sleep, though he knew she wasn't reading, but waiting. One morning there was a wonderful cactus on the breakfast table instead of delicate flowers. The cactus was in bloom. Its spikes were like long scorpion tails, with orange buds, sherbert color, on the tips, in wonderful contrast to the hard green of the skin and gray of the needles. He smiled, and she could tell behind their ordinary busy talk that something had touched him. But not enough. His vacuum was getting to be like a spiritual master, a place of tremendous calm and clarity that resisted any disturbance.

One morning the cactus was gone, and in its place were several kinds of shells, snail shells, sand dollars, white clam shells, burnished mother-of-pearl. The shells were in a crystal ashtray, one they had gotten in Ireland, though neither of them smoked. It had the family crest on the bottom, now hidden by the wonderful shapes of the shells. He lifted the sand dollar to experience once again how fragile it really was, never mind that it looked tough. And that was what she was saying to him. But the vacuum would not sustain palpable things. He knew his hand would do no harm to the shapes it touched. He knew he was a careful driver, never used his car as a weapon, never used language to hurt.

He laid the sand dollar very carefully back among the other shells and looked at her. And she saw his eyes were empty. He was perfectly present, but perfectly empty, and he was telling her this had happened, it was not a choice. And something rare appeared in her, a look that she was not defeated.

"No other way to say it," he thought, as he went to work. And there was a strange exhilaration in him that the vacuum could support. He saw the starlings flying again, in *M* shapes, *I* shapes, *S* shapes, as they flew towards or away from him.

One day soon after, at breakfast, instead of flowers or cactus or shells, there was a real hour glass. Where she got it he didn't know, it wasn't for timing boiled eggs. It had thin brass mounts and golden sand and a marvelous glass that was strikingly clear.

It was geometry in motion and it just matched his breakfast time, so with the last wipe of his mouth it was time to turn it. Then a few days later there was a small pendulum clock, the kind that swings in a circle, not back and forth in an arc, almost an effortless swing to the right, an easy stop, an effortless swing to the left. There was a crystal dome over it, and all the clock parts were displayed. It was a delight to him and she knew it.

Then after that there were small cards, done in gothic script, for she was very good at that, and on the cards were dates, dates he didn't recognize. He knew their wedding date, the birthdates of their children. But not these. Yet he began to notice they moved in progressions of twenty-eight days, more or less lunar intervals. The cards kept appearing until she knew he had guessed the intervals. Then came ones he knew almost immediately. Her birthday, her mother's birthday, her grandmother's birthday, but where did she get the ones going all the way back to 1823? Meantime their surface talk, their planning talk continued, and he continued to audit everything from brass bed posts to nose cones, and the children continued to rampage through breakfast and out to the school bus. Next there was a card with an "around" sign before the date, a future date, and he knew it was his, the end of his lifetime, and then he knew the one that was hers. The vacuum in him began to writhe, like the starlings again. But then it stopped. Instead it seemed to be standing like space over land and sea. He seemed to be standing on a sand dollar, and it did not give way. All the forms she had presented seemed to be holding him. There was a panic in him. He feared that the forms would give way and he would just drop, would start to fall and never stop falling.

One evening on the way home from auditing he stopped at a florist's shop where he spotted a blossoming camellia plant in the window. He explained he would pay for the bush but he wanted only one of the open white flowers. He knew there was a small Irish crystal fruit bowl at home. When he came in she was serving the children the junk food they craved, but she had some gourmet stuff in the oven—he could smell the herbs above the catsup. So he took the fruit bowl, filled it with water, unwrapped the camellia and floated it, then put the bowl in the middle of the junk food rampage on the kitchen table and went to hang up his things. The children thought he was simply doing something she had asked. When he came back in, the children, the water, the bowl were gone, but the flower lay face up in the middle of the debris on the table. She had dipped its face in the water, and it was beaded with perfect drops that kept their own clarity against the white face of the flower. So he knew she wanted no submission. And he knew one more thing. That she had been a vacuum long before him. And this was her solution.

30. Beliefs that Kill

For the Third Sunday of Easter

Then I heard every created thing in heaven and on earth and under the earth and in the sea, all that is in them, crying:
"Praise and honour, glory and might, to him who sits on the throne and to the Lamb for ever and ever!"
APOCALYPSE 5:13

A man was standing on the shore of the Lake of Galilee one day. He was sick of lies. He was sick of religion. Lies and religion were almost the same after his two-week tour of the Holy Land. Whose footprint was in this stone, who went up, who came down, whose grave, whose cradle? There was a bang a hundred yards away. His bus had been blown up, the one that brought him with a group of young Bible students from Jerusalem. The driver had been out in front of it. He did a couple of unplanned cartwheels and landed on his knees in the thick grass, scared but unscratched, looking at his bus, the rear end of which was in flames. No one was hurt, but everyone could have been if the timing of the bomb had been different.

"Stand back!" voices shouted. "Stand back!"

And sure enough, there were more explosions from the fuel tank, and soon the bus was like a burning skeleton. It took a while for a kibbutz fire department to show, but they did the right thing, checking to see if anyone was inside, no, anyone hurt outside, no, was everyone present, yes, would you get in a group and no one leave, yes. Then they put out what remained of the fire in what remained of the bus. By this time the military had come and they were looking for causes once they too found out there were no casualties. So the group was asked to sit in the grass on the Mount of Beatitudes up some hundred yards from the lake shore and parking lot and chapel were Jesus was supposed to have called Peter his "rock" and built his church on Peter's faith. The young man sat next to two teenagers, young college students, a man and a woman.

The young man kept saying, "Holy mackerel!" and the young woman kept trying to say something but nothing came out.

Over and over again the military ascertained the exact number on the bus, got the passports of those who still had them, got cross checks on those who had left them in luggage aboard. There had been several older people like the man who had joined the tour because there were seats free. But they had passports and were vouched for by the tour guide and the driver. So the source of the bomb was not in the group. Military buses would soon come and take them back to their hostels in Jerusalem.

"I came here to pray, to meet the Lord," the young man said.

And the young woman suddenly screamed at a soldier, "What have you done to the Lord's land? The bomb was for you, not for us!"

"No," the soldier said, "the bomb was for you. The mess was for me. They wanted me to have to scrape you off those rocks there. And they would take photos. And your home town would then be cursing me the way you are ready to right now. And cut off my money. So I would have no guns. Then someone could come in easily and make a mess out of me."

The young woman was speechless again.

The older man said to the soldier, "You're the first person I've heard in two weeks try to tell the truth."

The young man interrupted them all by saying, "The Lord prevented it from happening to us."

"You were lucky," said the military man.

"Then so were you," said the older man. "You don't know how lucky. This would have killed tourism here for a long while."

"We're not tourists," said the young man. "And this place has been profaned. We have to pray it back to being sacred."

He moved into a larger group and began to gather people to pray against the profanation of the place. The young woman for some reason couldn't move. She wanted to. She knew she was unharmed. She kept looking at her hands, her arms, her legs. It was as if she were seeing them as bits and pieces.

"Don't," said the military man. "The angel of death brushes by us many times. When he does not brush anymore you do not know it."

"You are both made of stone," she said.

The older man simply reached down and urged her to her feet. "Life is precious to me," he said, "whether you think so or not."

"And you too would kill to save it," the military man said.

"Not any more," the man said.

A hardness seemed to develop between the two men. Two people who had no fear of death.

The military man said, "When the bus comes I will see you on it. You will be safe until the next time." And he left to do more checking.

"You have both killed," said the young woman. "You know one another. What are you doing on this mount, on this lake? This belongs to the Lord of Peace!"

"No it does not," the man said. "You only think it does. Will you look beyond the bus to the Horns of Hattin, those two conelike mountains west of us? Do you know that a Crusader army was cut off from the water by a Saracen army? And the Crusaders went mad with thirst and ran for the lake but were cut down before they reached it? Do you know this land is so soaked with blood that there is a legend that says it has become a sacrificial victim, enough to save us all from our sins?"

"They were fighting for God!" the young woman said.

"Who?" the man said.

And the young woman looked shocked at the question, as if it was just a trick he was playing on her. "I'm going to pray with the group," she said. "Pray against the profanation of this land by those who don't believe." And she left the man.

He thought she didn't invite him to come. He was judged and found wanting.

"And I am," he thought. "I shot first in my own war and asked questions later. But there was no answer later. This is the answer here, a bomb on a bus, a group praying a psalm written by a bloody-minded man. To purify this lovely place. And a free trip home in an army vehicle."

"I prayed for you," the young woman said.

Her presence startled him a bit. He had wandered to the edge of the water and was looking at it ripple blue and silver in the light wind over the rocks of Peter.

"Well, thank you," he said, "not many do."

"Have you really killed people?"

"Yes, in one of America's wars."

She relaxed as if to say, "Then that's okay." And he looked at her and tears began to come down his face.

"It's not okay," he said, but he said it very gently so it would not be an argument. He rubbed the tears away with his hand.

The military man had come up to them just then to say, "You'll have to go in trucks. The way we do when we have to. Buses are not available. But we have mats so you won't be uncomfortable." He was looking straight at the man whose face was still wet, who did not flinch as he looked back at the military man. And there was that same stalemate as between two people who had no fear of death and no fear of inflicting it.

"It's not okay to kill," the older man said to the young woman, "even if we do." He was looking at the military man, who said, "I had to. You did not."

"And they have to," the older man said pointing to the bus.

"Me, yes. You, no," the military man said.

"It's my gun you have," the older man said.

"And you'd kill one another if you had to," the young woman

said. "So what are either of you doing here? Where are those trucks?" she said, "so that we can travel like you when *you* have to."

Neither of the two men moved. Something was gripping them and holding them, something they would never be able to say.

"Well, you can stay here," she said. But she didn't move either.

"Now we go," the military man said.

They fell in on either side of the young woman. And as they walked she too understood something that she would never be able to say.

31. Breaking Out

For the Fourth Sunday of Easter

For these are our instructions from the Lord: "I have appointed you to be a light for the Gentiles, and a means of salvation to earth's farthest bounds."

Acts 13:47

There was a woman who married out of her faith into another. Her husband was an intense, involved kind of person. He seemed to take life on like a chef in a great hotel that had to keep customers coming back for the menu alone. And she loved the clatter of it, the variety, the good taste of his living.

She took his faith as part of the excitement, though after a while she saw it was just another dish to him, not much of what it held influenced his life. So she began to live it for itself. There was a great compassion at the base, a great sense of forgiveness and a sense of reaching everyone in the world. But the funny thing was, the more she understood about his faith, the more she recognized that her husband and people like him, holy men included, were very hard toward other beliefs, very unforgiving. In fact the faith was like a wall they had built for themselves, with doorways in and out for commerce and pleasure, yes, but those doors were slammed on anything else.

"I'd be dead to them if I went back to my own faith," she thought. "As I'm dead to my own faith now!"

The day she realized this was a shocking day in her life. And a day of tremendous surprise, because she also recognized the genius of nonbelief, how it allowed people a certain universality, though it made them lesser beings in the eyes of believers, it made them like people in limbo.

"Limbo, that's it," she thought. "It's where the innocent babies go, and the good atheists." She remembered her Dante from school. So she left her husband, though it was war to do so, because he saw her as his property and was ready to ruin her rather than let her free. There was one great scene when he consigned her to the hell of the damned. He didn't really believe in such things, but it was a moment of fierce emotional release, to be rid of such trash as she, knowing that divinity would vindicate him against her forever.

She was in limbo all right. She went back to teaching special ed, the job for which she had been trained, dealing with the severely handicapped. It paid little and took a lot. But she began to pursue this limbo world with a passion she hadn't known she had. Believers called it secular humanism and sneered. There were the whales to care for. She spent a lot of hours listening to recordings of their voices. Then there were the unborn humans and what looked to her like a terrible slaughter, but she got caught there between the upper and nether millstones of fanatic belief and fanatic—what? "I don't know," she thought, "fanatic choosers?" Then there was the acid rain and visions of what it did to green fields and forests and lakes. Then there were the great famines with their terrifying toll on women and children.

"This is no limbo," she thought to herself one day, "A little more of this and my ex-husband will have his wish, I'll be in hell for good!" And that was the day of another great shock, for she knew you had to be God to live in limbo, at least the kind she knew. And you had to choose a menu.

"Maybe I'll start my own religion," she thought. "Call it 'Watch,' call myself a 'Watcher.' Good ring to that name, sounds heavy and serious and people won't think of a timepiece after a while. Maybe they won't think of witches either, or clothes in a machine." She saw the crossfire she would get into almost immediately. Or she'd be isolated like a germ, and anyone who joined her would be pariah.

"There it is, from another belief, pariah. It's limbo in another language. This is crazy. I should like someone who's wearing a skirt but instead she makes me jealous. I won't start another religion. I'll just have to go back to my own church and hope that it stretches."

She went back into a chapel one day. It was downtown, not far from the medical center where she worked, and was attached to a cloistered monastery.

"Walls," she thought, "and they're not made of rubber." After she got used to the shade and the quiet of the place she noticed a statue of a nun whose face and hands were the only parts of her showing—the rest was wimple, veil, and gown. But the statue had in her hand a heart, which she was holding out for everyone to see.

"Oh, it looks like a chicken liver," the woman thought. "And that body looks as if she's ashamed of it."

Then her eyes picked up a visionary bas relief up above the altar, the same nun kneeling looking up at Jesus descending from an altar, and there was ecstasy flowing from him and enveloping her. And the woman could see where the heart in the first statue's hands had come from.

"Is this the best we can do? They'd laugh at this in Singapore!" she thought.

"Somebody, somebody," she said out loud, "can't we do better than this?"

She noticed a lot of flowers up around the altar. There was no one else but herself. She had some adhesive tape in her bag, and a roll of bandages. So she got up very quietly and went to the front of the chapel, up to the altar. She snipped off a single rose, a nice open one, with big, big petals. She went over to the statue, dragged one of the priest's seats near it so she could climb, put the rose right over the ear of the statue, and fastened it there with tape. She went back and took a parrot's beak flower and taped it to the hand holding the heart so that the heart disappeared and what looked like a bird showed. Then she took out the roll of bandages and wrapped it around the head of the statue so that the eyes were covered, like Lady Justice, but also like the searcher in blind man's buff. Then she put a square of tape over the mouth.

"Now," she thought, "that's really Christianity. It's a love that's trapped. I'll be flung in jail for this. I'd better clean up." She reached up and pulled the tape gently off the mouth of the statue.

"Oouucchh," said a voice softly behind her. It was a contemplative nun who had come out from behind the grille to see if the woman was crazy. The woman took the rose off the statue's ear, the blindfold off its eyes, the parrot's beak out of its hand, working swiftly like a thief caught with the evidence.

"I'll buy you some new flowers," she said.

"They're really gifts," said the nun. "But you really made that statue say something else."

"Only for a minute," said the woman. "We're back where we were ten minutes ago. So much for my influence on our belief. What are you doing out of your cage?"

"Just to check if you were crazy or not. Have to bend the rule for crazies. They can harm themselves. Statues you can order by mail. Somebody makes these things overnight. We lost three last year. One to a slingshot, you wouldn't believe it, and ball bearings. The man stood in back and shot until he had chunks out of it and the bearings were bouncing all over the place. Freud would have loved that one.

"Another time somebody came in with cans of spray paint, somebody really good, and painted in breasts and belly button and crotch and knees so we had a Rio carnival dancer.

"The third time was kind of bad. Someone hung a mason jar of fetuses from her hand and broke it off. Where they got them I don't know, but we were sick for weeks. This place does things to people. And it's only an old chapel."

"Then that puts me with the crazies," said the woman.

"No," said the nun, "it's the same problem wherever you stand. Things can't speak for themselves." The nun reached for the rose in the woman's hand and slid it inside her cowl just at the ear. Then she took the parrot's beak and held it in her left hand.

"We'll do without the blindfold and the adhesive tape," she said. Then she gave the woman a kiss on the cheek and a kind of hug, back patting style. "I'm your statue, now take care of yourself." And she went back inside her cage. And the woman left the chapel with a new religion.

32. No More Bullshit

For the Fifth Sunday of Easter

> They warned them that to enter the kingdom of God we must pass through many hardships. They also appointed elders for them in each congregation, and with prayer and fasting committed them to the Lord in whom they had put their faith.
>
> ACTS 14:22–23

There was a man who had no principles. Life had none, he thought, so why should he? He liked life, he was privileged, good mind, good money, good looks. So he wasn't out to take revenge on anyone or anything. He made sure people were pleased when he got what he wanted from them. When he reached his fifties, though, he began to become invisible, as if life existed somewhere else or he was a curiosity, playing a young game with an old frame.

Lately his money was more sought than his mind. A beggar world came up to him, watching its own palm and what he put in it, not him. But he was ready for this shift, because he knew life had no principles. It dawned on him he could make a private crusade out of that, it would spice up the latter part of his life, to go around denuding people of their illusions.

"But it's got to be better than that," he thought. "It can't be just revenge, that's no fun. It's got to be like the dawning of the truth. That marvelous joke about the city kid and his father, with the father teaching the kid to be street-wise. 'Climb up that wall and jump and I'll catch you,' says the father. 'No,' says the son, 'You'll step back and let me hit the ground!' 'Oh son,' says the father, 'would I do that to my own flesh and blood?' 'Okay,' says the kid, all thrilled. The boy climbs on the wall and one, two, three, jumps. The father steps back and lets him hit the ground. And the kid cries. The father soothes him, but says, 'See, don't even trust your own father!' And the two walk off together hand in hand." The two walking off together was the best part of the joke.

So he began to attend all kinds of meetings for charitable causes. And he came impeccably dressed with the aura about him of the rich world he came from. It didn't square with the people who worked for those causes, but they had to be nice to him, and he had extraordinarily well-informed questions for them to answer. And counter pleas. He would ask them in turn to contribute to country club expansion drives, or drives for a new wing for an art museum. This was after he donated well to the charitable cause. He signed petitions for all kinds of environmentalists, then handed out petitions for zoning changes for them to sign, changes that would allow nuclear dumps in this place or that. Well, the anger level in all this became a little too hot for comfort.

"Nobody's disabused," he thought, 'The illusions intensify."

One woman caught on to what he was doing, that is to say, why. "You want everyone to know nothing really matters," she said to him one day at a Bread For The World meeting.

"Nothing does," he said, "and that's not my doing."

"Whose doing is it?" she asked.

"Life's," he said. "But I love life, don't get me wrong. It's that I'm at a point where the big trick has been pulled on me and I'm looking for companionship."

"Companions are a dime a dozen," she said.

"I mean someone who sees what I see," he said. "That's the big trick life pulls on you. If you're alone you go out."

"And if you have a companion?"

"You go out too, pun and all."

"This is the wrong place to look," the woman said. "These people believe in saving even scraps of life."

"It's the right place," the man said. "This is where the disillusion can set in quickest. Idealists also come to terrible ends."

"You're a lot of bullshit."

"Exactly. Now tell me what you are."

"I'm a killer."

"You wouldn't just tell me straight like that," the man said. "There must be a story. You're not a gun for hire."

"Drunk driving," she said. "A woman and a baby carriage in a park. I thought the park was a street."

"So this is your sentence," the man said, "To work for charities like this."

"Yes," she said, "several. Takes a lot of time. But my husband and children don't have to come and get me off someone's floor."

"So you live at home, not some jail."

"No, they have their own lives now. What they're glad of is that I have mine."

"Well, that's no bullshit," the man said. "It's a different kind of trick."

"Don't say it." She put her hand through his arm and moved him toward the door. "You don't go out," she said. "You go deeper into some kind of a hell. There isn't any finish to this. Even when you're cold as a mackerel."

"That isn't something you can know," he said.

She kept her hand in his arm. "Just walk me, like your prize poodle."

So they walked, and he knew she was really holding on, though he was free to quit and go.

"How do you like your companion?" she asked.

"She scares me. She thinks you don't go out, you just go deeper."

"Have you ever drunk because you had to?" she asked.

"No."

"Then I can't tell you," she said. "Have you ever done anything you had to? Apart from cleanness and sleep and food?"

"No," he said. "I always choose, apart from the things you said."

"Then I can't tell you," she said again. "How about this not wanting to be alone, the big trick of life?"

He couldn't say anything. Because he now knew he could not stop looking. "I don't think I can be alone in this," he said.

"Then I think I can explain," she said. "In a minute."

She stopped and seemed to shake for a while. "You see, if they're dead for good . . ." She couldn't finish the sentence.

She started another. "If you want oblivion, you have to create it, and if the means fail, if the drink doesn't get you there . . ." She couldn't finish again.

"Then you're thirsting for something nobody has."

They were walking again.

"That's where your trick is, isn't it?" she said. "The illusion."

"Yes," he said, "exactly. But I want someone who knows it."

"For what?" she said.

He said nothing.

"So you won't disappear?" she said. "You'd love it like this for good. But that's not what the thirst is. You see if they're dead for good and I did it . . ." She couldn't finish. "And I have no way to forget . . . then I'll remember," she said, "and I won't go out."

"That's pure defiance," he said.

"No," she said, "it's the counter-trick. Nobody laughs down the barrel of a gun. But it slakes my thirst, I tell you. I'm not holding you like a drink."

"There'll be an end to it," he said. "Maybe somebody else drunk behind a wheel, I hope not. Maybe just a plain old death in a plain old bed."

"No. There's no end to a thirst. I tried to tell you. And nobody can stay alone."

"That's where I started with you," he said, "and we've walked and we haven't gotten any further."

"Then I can't explain. And that will make me a good companion for you."

"You're a lot younger than I am."

"You need someone old? So you go out together? What if I agree to jump off the wall the same time you do?"

This time he stopped. His joke had turned suddenly sour in his memory. "You got me," he said. "I'd be your drunk driver."

She still had her arm in his and he could feel her jolt. "Didn't mean it," he said.

"No, you didn't," she said. "I think I felt them even if I was drunk out of my mind."

He started to walk again. "Tell you what. I have nothing to lose."

"And nothing to gain."

"Exactly, nothing to gain."

They were near a bar, so he said, "How about a drink?" And they both stood there until she laughed.

"But you've got a lot to learn," she said. "I mean a lot."

33. Old Dog, New Tricks

For the Sixth Sunday of Easter

Peace is my parting gift to you, my own peace, such as the world cannot give.

JOHN 14:27

"When you're young," a man said, "you believe in the resurrection of the body. When you're old, you believe in the immortality of the soul. That is if you believe in anything." He said this to a woman who was painting a picture of irises in oils.

"Mmm," said the woman with a brush in her mouth and her eyes on a daub of purple she was trying to lighten.

"You can run like a dog when you're young," he said, "saliva and all. Makes perfect sense to last forever."

"Mmm," said the woman again, and motioned him to move the vase of irises a little in from the window of the studio.

"Too much light?" he asked.

"Mmm," she said.

"You're like an upside down turtle when you're old. I saw an old oriental man near the library yesterday. He was running downhill, an inch an hour. He was in bliss. A gust of wind knocked him over. Slow motion. He loved it. His daughter had to pick him up."

"Mmm," said the woman and sat there puzzled between the irises and the painting.

"Too little light?" the man said as he moved the irises back toward the window. "Here?" he asked.

"Mmm," she said in approval and began to lay down strokes of just the right purple.

"We used to make love like a hurricane hit us," the man said. "Outside of time. With all the glockenspiels playing. You used to worry the kids would read a book about sex or find out about it on the street and our happy home would be a crate of broken eggs. It's been so long I have amnesia."

"Mmm," said the woman as she switched brushes. She had three of them in her mouth and she looked like a triple pirate from a silent movie, except she would daub her cheek at each change of brush, so she looked like a cave painting too, lots of dots on a rugged surface.

"That's the soul," he said. "Nice even line on the heart machine. No blip, blip. You're like that when you don't remember."

"Mmm," she said, and it was sad.

"Your mother," he said.

"Mmm," she said, and she began to put in touches of white in the throats of the irises, watching carefully to see if they were light enough. Oils were hard to manage. But oils lasted.

"She couldn't remember the last word," he said. "What a silence that was. I catch it in myself sometimes. I'm looking at a damn menu and don't know what leek soup is until my mouth waters to tell me and then I remember. That's why I say, when the body leads you, it's time for resurrection, when the soul does, it's time for immortality. You want some tea?"

"Mmm," the woman said with anticipation as she began to squeeze green out of her tube for the stems.

"Argh," the man said as he got up slowly. "I'm like a medieval clock. Grease won't help." He put his hand on her shoulder to steady himself and used the moment to look at the painting.

"Ah," he said, 'it looks like one you stepped on. But you have funny ways. They come out looking better than themselves. Back in a second." And he moved slowly out of the studio into the kitchen. The kettle rattle-banged in the sink.

"Too much water," he muttered for her. "Boil a whole lake." Then he punched some buttons on the electric stove. "It's like punching your future," he giggled. "Nothing happens for five minutes. Better not touch to find out. Bags," he said. "You want it strong?"

"Mmm," she said through the door.

Now all the brushes were in her mouth as she moved the spatula to mix the green to a lighter shade.

"I'll have to lug you to the toilet in half an hour," he said.

She kept concentrating on the color.

"Okay, two bags full," he said. Then he giggled again. "That's us."

He said nothing for a while, just clattered the cups and pot, then said, "And we are full." There was a whistle from the kettle. Not much of a one.

"It's a sick bird," he said, "don't pick it up. Let the hawks get it. Or a stupid dog. Cycle of nature."

There was a slight hiss as he poured the water in to heat the pot. Then a sloshing sound. Then a pouring sound.

"Great pot," he said. "Those buttercups you painted on it look like they're going to kiss you if you get too close."

He took down the tea tin that kept the bags fresh. Had trouble getting it open. "Quick, quick," he said to himself, "time is a thief."

The lid sprang across the floor and bounced clackety-clack under the breakfast table. "A half an hour on my knees to get that damn thing," he said to her. "Like a spelunker looking for a way out. Okay, one bag for you, one for me, and one for the pot. In with the water, on with the lid, and nobody move. Except me," he said as he rattled the tray together, milk and sugar and tea biscuits, adding the cups and saucers that matched the pot with the buttercups.

"Here I come," he said, "the next crash you hear will be me if I don't make it. Call the friendly undertaker, the one who gives green stamps."

When he got back inside the studio she was weeping silently, looking at him, not the irises. The brushes were still in her mouth.

"That was too cute," he said to her. "I play with it so I can make believe I'm bigger."

He put the tea down, took a paper napkin and dried her wet eyes. Then he took the brushes out of her mouth, poured tea, mixed in milk and sugar, then put the cup within reach of her hand.

"You've just got a few things left, you can do ten times as much as I can," he said.

He took his own cup. There was a slight rattle to it. "For two bits, what is it, a cold or a fever?" he said.

"Mmm," she said as she tasted the tea.

"When I was a kid," he said, "and first heard the words St. Vitus Dance, I thought it was fantastically mystical. Like that other, St. Elmo's fire. I've got a little of both and I don't feel so mystical."

The woman was looking at the irises again. She took one more sip to finish her tea, then reached for a brush and began to touch the painting quickly. She took another brush and worked quickly in another color, then another brush, another color. Time seemed suspended. He sipped from his empty cup he was so absorbed.

Finally she paused and leaned back in her chair, the wicker chair she liked because it responded with its own sounds to her movement.

"It's alive," he said. "Nobody stepped on that. What will you do for a background?"

She reached for the tube of gold, unscrewed the cap with one hand, put a dab of it on the paint board and studied it.

"Don't let any Van Gogh sneak in," he said.

She laughed and put the cap back on.

"Okay, later," he said. "A few more of these oils and you'll have enough for a show. I'll give Simons a call and have him save space. He's a greedy guy. Think I see teeth marks on his checks. So a nap?"

"Mmm," she said.

"Okay, hook a ride," he said.

She rose very slowly, one side limp, but the other not, and put the good arm around his shoulder, giving his hair a brush back as she did.

"Careful," he said, "it comes out."

She paused to look at the painting again, to see it from a different angle.

"It's good," he said. "Even the vase looks like it could break. What will I read?" he said, as they went slowly toward the den and her Queen Anne chair. "A book on dogs or a book on ghosts?"

He giggled a bit. "I'm going to read to you a new translation of *Sir Gawain And The Green Knight*. It's by an old student of mine. The scene in the hall where the Green Knight picks up his chopped-off head, says 'See you in a year,' and rides out of the hall. Wonderful stuff. And if you're still awake, I'll read the seduction scene from later."

"Mmm," said the woman and settled in her chair.

34. Hidden Miracles

For the Seventh Sunday of Easter

> I made thy name known to them, and will make it known, so that the love thou hadst for me may be in them, and I may be in them.
>
> JOHN 17:26

There was a missionary who knew he was finished. The doctor's report had come up to the mountain village. It gave him maybe a year to live. There was no going home, he was old, and had been out so long no one home knew him much. They only knew he was a great linguist, had learned several difficult Indian tongues, and was a great mountain man. He could travel where no one else would. Had found people and brought them health and the message, each to take as they pleased. And had learned stories he could tell by the hour from many peoples. If anyone would listen.

In the last few years he had almost ceased to be a missionary. He did all the rituals people wanted, yes, but he seemed more like one of the great eagles who passed overhead or swooped downslope after a hare, or just floated with its partner right in the eye of the sun, sometimes brushing wings in counter circles, sometimes tumbling hundreds of feet, claw locked to claw in magnificent airmanship. His mountain people knew that if he had wings . . . but no human has.

So they watched him, or watched for him, because they feared he would harm himself, fall in a ditch while watching the sky, or forget he was on a face of a rock and let go to reach for the incredible wild flowers that grew in the spring on the rock faces of the mountains. The town was close to those cliffs. Good eyes could see every movement on them, especially the movements of the mountain goats. Then the villagers would dash to try to catch a few for their meat, hide, and horns.

The missionary was like a goat in that he ate anything put in front of him, and they loved to feed him—it was like feeding the earth back for what it fed them. Well, he told them about his short time to live, and they were grieved in a deep silence which he understood. "I'm going to meet it," he told them, "the way the old people did here before Christ came." Some knew what he meant, others did not, but no one spoke since it would be soon enough they would find out. So for a time he kept going the way he always had. But people changed their customs a bit toward him. People would put a stone down on his shadow when he walked by. And they would never let their shadows cross him. But they always touched him as they passed to his right or left, depending on where their shadows fell. They brushed him with their fingers as if to take something from him. He knew they were fighting death for him. And it filled him with a love he could not express.

After a few bad nights when he could keep nothing down, he knew there would be a steep and quick descent. So in the morning in this east/west valley he left the missioner's house and walked toward the face of the mountain just to the west, his shadow long before him from the sun that had just appeared, not a sharp shadow since the earth was still misty behind him. And then he began to climb the face, not in his usual jeans and boots, but in his cassock. People noticed and came into the streets. They noticed the route he took up the sheer rock wall— one you could go up but not come down. All that long morning they watched the black figure inch upward with consummate skill but clearly a lack of great strength. He paused often. But never looked back. They were sure he would tumble and there would be little left to look at when he hit bottom. But he didn't fall. Finally, there was a moment when two eagles flapped free of a shelf, screaming and swinging in anger and diving at him. It was too early for them to have young but it was their customary place. The people saw the black figure hook over the lip of the shelf and disappear.

They did not see him again. For days they watched. And the eagles kept swinging by the place, screaming at him. Then one day they were driven off by condors. The condors landed on the rock shelf, and the people knew the priest was gone. They sensed the earth was taking him back and giving him the wings he had never had. After many days the condors stopped coming. The eagles returned but still did not alight, just swept past, this time making no noise. Then one day a violent earthquake shook the valley and much of the mountain face broke off and came crashing down toward the village, but went to either side of it in roars of gravel and bounding boulders. The village had been built on a small breast-like hill, and the rock fell around it like a horseshoe and seemed to bury the stream that had run around the rock-fall. The people thought they would be without water, but after a few days they knew it was not so. The stream had been made into a chain of cisterns, and as they filled the water began to spill from one cistern to the next, until there was a rock-studded lake on three sides of the village, not a large one, but one that would retain water during the dry summer.

Then they saw the eagles. The rock shelf where their nest was had not fallen, but was even more difficult of access than before. It was mating season. And the people saw them mate and begin to repair their nest. So he must be entirely gone, they thought. And he had done this, he had saved this place and surrounded it with water. So they began to work with shadows. A whole custom of greeting one another began. They would move their shadows consciously across one another. They began to stand near places where their hands could talk in images on walls. Not much talk. They began to arrange shapes of the earth so they intersected in patterns, daily as well as seasonal. And they would often stand at the edge of a place and allow the shadow of the mountain to creep over them like a tide. They found distinctive ways of weaving their clothing in new patterns of black and white, patterns that imitated the effects of the sun on the world they lived in.

Nights became a precious thing for them. They married only at night, and for the time of joining they extinguished all lights, and the guests waved fans slowly in the new home, so that soft air circulated, and then they left the couple. The wedding festivity took place at dawn in a wild shadow dance against the face of the changed mountain just as the sun came red over the rim of the east end of the valley.

When priests came to visit, the villagers asked for changes. They wanted midnight for baptism. At the pouring of the water the lights would go out and the air would stir. And they wanted mass in the open, where the shadows of several forms crossed. The priests often felt the movement of people which seemed aimless, but they were always shadowed in some way, someone on a roof just so, someone on a rock just so, except at high noon masses which were for the great feasts, when everyone seemed to yield their shadows to the absolute light. Most priests went along with this. Some didn't, and the services seemed to be very cold and the people very patient.

One morning the people found the male eagle at the bottom of the mountain face. They buried it. And they watched the female until she disappeared. They knew for sure that the old priest had left them behind. It was shortly thereafter that tough people began to show up on the edge of town, people looking for something. More and more they hunted through the rock-fall that surrounded the village, down into the sands that had formed in the natural cisterns. They found what they were looking for, the gold flakes which showed the mountain was veined with the precious metal. The people had no title to the land. Army units moved in as if onto government property. Then larger and larger equipment. The people were moved out to the east end of the valley to tend their fields, which were in the middle. They had to reverse their shadow life, and their customs changed. They watched their former home turn into a forest of drills and a maelstrom of sound.

One day the earth shook again, this time terribly and long. And the rest of the face of the mountain came down, including the eagle's shelf. By a miracle again no one was hurt since the great shaking came at night, but the equipment was buried and huge pieces of cliff seemed to totter above the place where the work had gone on, as if a sneeze would bring it down on the rest of the rubble. So the people knew the missionary had not gone. And it was confirmed the day the eagle returned with a new mate. They watched it circle over their old place and find nothing it wanted. Then they watched it and its mate sweeping north to south back down the valley toward themselves. Then high above their heads on the east wall the pair seemd to settle. And the people were sure.

Over time the village was studied. The priests had spread word about the invention of new myths. But now tender people came who watched them and wrote about them, but no one asked them why, just how. So the villagers showed them how. Then they understood what the priest had done for them. He had put them also out of reach. Like the gold.

35. A Lesson for Fanatics

For Pentecost Sunday

For all who are moved by the Spirit of God are sons of God. The Spirit
you have received is not a spirit of slavery leading you back into a life of
fear, but a Spirit that makes us sons, enabling us to cry "Abba! Father!"
ROMANS 8:14–15

There was a woman who was psychic. She could tell what people
were and what they could do. Not immediately, they had to talk
to her first. But once they did she could see. It was as if fog lifted
and landscapes or seascapes were exposed. And they didn't have
to say much. She had solved most of the problems of how to live
with this power, mainly by never admitting to it, or never living
off it, but by using it always indirectly, giving advice, or being in
the right place at the right time for someone. But one problem she
had never solved. Fate. People seemed fated to do certain things.
She had been right so often that now she lived in fear that no one
was really responsible, that everyone followed patterns set out for
them.

Ironically, she could not read herself. She had tried for years,
but the message always came back, "You are not to know." She
had married because she loved the man, and had had her children
because she loved creating them. But she saw their fates, too, day
in and day out, and made every secret attempt she could to struggle with those fates, but their lives went on as if without her, and
all she knew of herself was that she could love more and more
deeply as they grew or went on living.

One day she recognized that her husband was under someone's
orders to kill her and make it look like an accident. In torment, he
tried to conceal his plan by saying certain of his clients were in
tough legal situations. He was a criminal lawyer. She had met
some of his clients, clean and wealthy, or dirty and poor.

"I know something," she thought. "And someone knows I
know. And has power over my husband. Which means he has

done something wrong, or is vulnerable in some way. And this is the price he has to pay. My life for his."

She sat for a long time visualizing scenes when she had met people with him. Finally she came to one. It had been a political fundraiser, a dinner. She had met the candidate and his wife. The wife had said some things. As she listened, the woman's psychic powers revealed a grisly story to her. The candidate's wife had killed people and was ready to kill again. She had a history of terrorism under other names and some years back. And history was stretching ahead for her, though in a different form of killing, through a political figure if he got elected. If not, she would divorce him and find another way.

The psychic woman thought, "My face must have showed what I saw, my poor face. And that other woman saw herself naked. Now what has she got on him?"

It was not long before she knew: his nationality—his relatives still lived in the home country. The candidate had been elected to a national office. His influence was potentially great. And the casualty rate would be high.

"So before I blow the whistle" the woman thought, but didn't finish the sentence, because her husband came into the living room, just home from the office, with an eager look about him, a fake eager look.

He pulled from both pockets of his trenchcoat some travel brochures for the Caribbean, dumped them on the coffee table, and said, "If I don't get some sun soon, I'll petrify. Here, look these over, find a week's trip somewhere. The kids can afford to lose some school, they've been coughing for a month. I have to make a call. See if there's something."

She knew he had decided to kill her. She knew she could not know if he would succeed. So she spread the folders in front of her and gave them a quick glance, waiting until he came back from his call. He was rattling a drink and sank into a chair across from her as if too tired to taste it. She knew that was a fake too.

"I know everything," she said, "except if you will succeed or not. On this island, you have the best chance. It's still primitive and people can be paid to say sharks did it, or the scuba equipment got caught on coral, or the old truck simply had no brakes. What I don't know is if you are willing to lose the children too, under that truck."

He sat there and he *was* petrified.

"So it isn't just blackmail; you must believe in their cause," she continued. "So here is what we do. You either kill me in this room now with your own two hands, or we go to the FBI and say clearly who she is and what pressure she's putting on our beloved congressman."

She saw him casting around in his mind for alternatives, ways of making it look like an accident. She saw the love for her was gone, replaced by whatever cause he had embraced. She was facing a killer. But one who knew that her murder would reveal the story quicker than anything else. He had no motive to kill her.

"I have an alternative for you," she said. "I will help you work against all deaths. You now know I can read people. You will tell them you have decided to work against all deaths. That if they kill anyone you will tell on them. And that you can find out through me. That you will not stop anything legal they do, only anything illegal."

"We're both dead that way," he said.

"Not if we record," she said.

"You are concealing a crime," he said. "It makes you a criminal too."

"Who is to judge that?" she said. "Certainly not you."

"I can't live with you," he said.

"You don't have any choice," she said. "You're my one way to uncover these people."

She saw the rage rising in him, an impotent rage. He was boxed in on every side.

"If someone is going to use you," she said, "it might as well be me."

Then she saw he lacked the one thing necessary for a true fanatic. He was afraid to die—or he would have killed her on the spot.

"I have to phone," he said.

As soon as he left the room, she ran through the kitchen to her own car and sped out of the driveway. That forced him to make another phone call. She went to the public library and wrote out in detail all she knew of the people in his circle. Then she attached a note to it, to the local parish priest, calling it a case of conscience that she needed his help in solving. She addressed and stamped it and put it in the mail box outside the library. Then she drove home. He was there with the children—the school bus had just dropped them off. So they had to see to the feeding, the recreation, the disposition of the children for homework and bed before they were able to face one another again.

"You told someone," he said.

"Yes," she said, "in case anything happens to me. You'll at least lose your victim in Congress."

"They're going to take us both," he said. "It's only a question of time."

She heard the fate in his voice, the fate she had always feared.

"Then get off that chair and make sure that no more than ourselves die." She said this hissing in anger.

He understood that she had no fear of death, not at all, she was more intense than any of those who wanted her dead. And he saw that intensity as a way he could cling to what life was left. So he rose to go to the phone.

"No, not to them!" she said. "Later to them. You get in your car and drive. And from your car phone you tell all. And make sure you tell someone who has to record incoming calls. The feds will neutralize your congressman with no scandal, and all this gun stuff will stop for a while. And if I'm still here when you get back, there's a life I have to plan with you. And if they kill you out there or me here, they convict themselves."

He went out and drove off.

"A life to plan," she thought, "like stitching wounds all day and all night." But she felt her own fanaticism for the first time as a power to face death and make it change its ways. Not for worthy motives. Not yet. Maybe someday.

36. Stranded with God

Trinity Sunday

More than this: let us even exult in our present sufferings, because we know that suffering trains us to endure, and endurance brings proof that we have stood the test, and this proof is the ground of hope. Such a hope is no mockery, because God's love has flooded our inmost heart through the Holy Spirit he has given us.

ROMANS 5:3–5

A man and a woman were walking along a beach one evening. The wind was good, it didn't tear their words away, it cooled their faces and gave them a taste of salt on their lips.

"The tide is turning," he said. "Can you feel the pull?"

"Yes," she said, "and hear it, there's that nice rattle of shale being raked. It's so different from losing life."

"You mean losing it all of a sudden?"

"Yes. In a bomb or a crash."

"We shouldn't be thinking that here," he said. "It's almost a betrayal."

"I know, but this place repairs itself. You remember the storm that stripped it clean? There wasn't a pinch of sand left."

"Now it's flat and silky, and the sand ribs show through the water. Nice. Like a lean dog."

"That never happens to a body," she said. "The sea does not repair it. My father used to tell me about the banshees in Ireland wailing offshore when fishermen drowned and nobody knew. So the folk used to walk the strand waiting for the corpse to wash ashore."

"Did the bodies wash in?" the man asked her.

"My father told me they did," the woman said. "Then people would bless the sea for bringing the body back even if it had been cruel."

"I guess they knew they had to live with it or it would harm them more. That's the old paganism," the man said.

"A strange god," the woman said, "one who kills, then hands you back the corpse. I hope we have a better one."

"Do you wonder if we do?"

"Some days yes," she said, "when everything I love turns savage for some reason and shooting starts in the name of God or justice or retaliation or whatever people think holy."

The man said, "I remember one time I was caught in a riot in Paris, caught between the police and the students. The police were swinging their rubber truncheons like maniacs. I got in an alleyway just in time. I walked out later when things were calm, I saw a policeman wiping blood carefully off a student's face with a handkerchief, wetting it with his own saliva."

"That's just what I mean. Some days God is wiping away the blood."

"I think we're stuck with the wrong idea."

"We are," she said. "But everything we look at kills to cure. Like this great god sea."

"It's not killing now," he said. "Look up, how blue it is, and pink where the sun reflects. Those cormorants have found a school of fish."

"Do you think the killing will ever stop?" she asked him. "I'm almost in despair."

"Yes, it will."

"How do you know?"

"From your despair."

"What do you mean?"

"It goes against everything you are. It can't be right."

"That's sweet, but you must have bigger reasons."

"Like what?"

"Oh," she said, "like the real God, or Jesus on the cross, or the last judgment, or hell and damnation."

"Yes," he said, "but really no. It's pure logic. I think despair would ruin you. And if it ruined you, it would ruin me. And if it ruined me, there'd be no walking the beauty of this beach, then no looking at the sea, then nothing in the sky, then nothing. Despair makes nothing of everything."

"You lost me."

"I lost myself," he said. "I feel like those gulls out there wheeling around for a fish. The killing will stop because it has to. There's no life even in God if it goes on."

"I imagine that's right," she said. "You can't stop loving. There's nothing outside it. There, do I look better with hope?"

"Well," he said, "I can see more than the top of your head now."

"I've been watching us leave indelible footprints on the sands of time," she said.

"They'll know you've got big feet."

"No, they'll think a beauty was walking with a beast."

"You're right," he said, "but don't be down again. You're really a nice-looking beast."

37. Woman Makes Money Talk
For the Ninth Sunday in Ordinary Time

> Does my language now sound as if I were canvassing for men's support? Whose support do I want but God's alone? Do you think I am currying favor with men? If I still sought men's favour, I should be no servant of Christ.
>
> GALATIANS 1:10

There was a woman whose husband was being tried in a federal court. He was a bank official accused of laundering mob money. He had failed to report some large transfers. An oversight, he said. Complicity, the government said. The woman came to court with her husband. She stood outside in the corridor during a break while he conferred with his lawyers; she sat on one of those official benches as the life of justice went by her on hard or soft heels.

She had seen her own picture in the paper several times, walking just ahead of him into court. There she was, in a basket next to the ashtray. She had a navy suit and a choke collar on that day, and the cameo brooch she had bought near the Trevi Fountain.

"I'm bought too," she thought. "He laundered that money and

I'm wearing it." A sense of shame came over her that made her dizzy. She remembered the Watergate wives, all those women compromised by all those men. She wasn't a romantic. She remembered the women on trial later for their own lack of conscience. But they were really outnumbered by the men.

Several other trials were taking a break. None of them were crimes of passion, that she could see. Nobody on trial for a meatax murder or euthanasia. There was a big narcotics one, she knew, and a spy one, though small apples. And a congressman caught in an FBI scam. Then her own man for laundering money. A young woman sat beside her, half looking at her, not curious, just needy, with unspoken need. The older woman turned slightly toward the younger one as if to give her an opening. Suddenly there were camera flashes, and the young woman said, "Oh my God! I'm making it worse!" and she started up, but got only halfway before the force of the older woman's grip drew her back down to the bench.

"You're the spy's woman,"the older woman said. "I'm the thief's."

The young woman opened up as if she had been released from a cage. "I know," she said, "I feel so cut off. I thought you might know. But we'll be plastered all over the papers. And you'll look worse."

The older woman took the younger woman in her arms, and the younger one broke down and the flash bulbs went berserk.

"Come, let's wash up," the older one said. She took the younger one's arm and started for the ladies' room. They had to move around a group blocking a courtroom door. A woman coming out of the group bumped into them because she was looking over her shoulder saying, "Damn you!" to someone. She somehow got tangled up with the other two women, who had been arm in arm, and the rigidity of her body seemed to wilt against the softness of theirs. She backed up a bit and saw the two and knew them. The flash bulbs went berserk again.

"I'm the thief's wife," said the older woman. "This is the spy's. And we are going to wash up. Come on."

But the congressman's wife couldn't move for a minute, though she did put her hands out and grab hold of their open coats as if to form a corral of the three against the world. "Yes," she said, and without letting go she walked half sideways with them toward the ladies' room.

They could hardly get in the door because there were so many plainclothes police outside and more photographers. In fact the three women were searched before they could go in. Once inside they saw why: there was the star witness in the drug trial. She was as beautiful a blond woman as any of them had ever seen, dressed in impeccable, body-fitting black and white—black slacks and white cashmere turtleneck, with a black bead necklace. She was standing with her back to the mirror, frozen with fear. She saw the other three, and a slow look of recognition came over her face. How was this possible? The wives of a thief, a spy, a crooked congressman, and a drug dealer—she just opened her hands in front of her, like an actress, as if to say *Why?* And they all kind of moved into a huddle together. There was a great release of tension. A private kind of laughter began. The older woman started it, and gradually it became somewhat hysterical and mixed with tears, and the huddle got tighter.

Then the older woman backed away a bit and began to remove her clothing. "It's all stolen," she said. "I'm walking out of here clean. I'm going to do one clean thing." She placed all her things carefully in the sink and began to walk toward the door.

"Wait, we're all the same," said the crooked congressman's wife. So the other three undressed and began to move toward the door with the older woman.

But the drug dealer's woman said, "They'll mock us like fools. Why don't we just swap clothes. To say it doesn't matter what woman we are. We get screwed anyway." So they exchanged clothes, dressed, and moved through the door.

The police surrounded the woman with the cashmere turtleneck immediately, but when they saw she was wearing a skirt, they made a frenzied grab for the other three and found the blond woman in a gray suit coat. The police herded the four of them together, then in a flying wedge went through the crowd into the back of the drug case courtroom, pushed all four women against the wall, and said, "What the hell's going on? Who are you?"

"I'm the thief's wife," said the first woman.

"I'm the spy's," said the second.

"I'm the crooked congressman's," said the third.

"Goddamn, you're not," a police officer said. "You're after our witness."

"Goddamn I am," said the first woman. "Go get my husband in Courtroom Three."

So they got the thief and the spy and the crooked congressman, who all made the identification, so the police freed the women.

The women then decided to swap courtrooms. And everybody around began to notice it: the spy's woman was going to the thief's, the thief's to the crooked congressman's, the crooked congressman's to the spy's. The judges were furious because the flash bulbs were going off like crazy. The women were swapping clothes and changing hairdos, disappearing into the ladies' room and coming back out looking different. Until the verdicts began to come in, one by one, all guilty on charges of drugs, spying, corruption. The woman of the thief found herself the last, the older woman, now alone. Her man was guilty too. While he was huddling with his lawyers about appealing the sentence, she went to the ladies' room, took out a body stocking that went from her neck to her ankles, undressed, put it on, left her clothes, and walked out the door. The body stocking was like an allover tattoo. On her breasts were pictures of two crocodile mouths champing on dollar bills. On her pelvis was a picture of an open pocketbook, but inverted so coins and bills poured out and down her legs. Over her belly was a Susan B. Anthony silver dollar, and Susan was winking. Her buttocks were covered by a picture of a billfold opened so that credit cards moved up and down as she walked. The garment showed a picture of a blank check between her shoulder blades. And images of long sales slips marched down either arm with the totals at her wrists. She walked into the courtroom, and there was a furious scene, flashbulbs popping, her husband trying to rip the body stocking off her, people intervening, shoving her toward the door, out along the corridor, down the broad staircase, out into the street, where they left her.

She started to walk. There were smiles everywhere. There were voices. There were kids dancing around. There were horns honking, greetings, meetings, hootings. There were bums who got in line behind her. And photographers who ran ahead. The crocodiles champed, and the purse poured, and Susan B. Anthony winked, and the sales slips and the credit cards undulated to a different rhythm. "They know me," she thought. "If I took this off they wouldn't."

38. In the Saint Trade

For the Tenth Sunday in Ordinary Time

Then she said to Elijah, "Now I know for certain that you are a man of God and that the word of the Lord on your lips is truth."

1 KINGS 17:24

There was a man whose job it was to screen candidates for sanctity. Dead ones, of course. It was a church job, and he had to take a look at the dossiers when they first arrived and judge if they should be passed on for real scrutiny, or if they should be sent back politely with suggestions of difficulties.

A classic example was the concentration camp guard who, after the war, had a change of heart and did thirty years of penance and charity though no one knew why. The difficulty was, he had created his own tribunal and retained control of his own life, instead of submitting to the community and its judgment. If he were canonized a lot of people would forgive themselves and maybe not do the penance and charity.

A rarer case was that of a woman from a high valley in the Andes of South America who spent her life trying to transform the condition of women in her region. Her fiancé had been killed in a stupid war. She had lived unmarried, had brought up several orphans from her own family, had written remarkable poetry, had begun the first school for young women, and had died much revered some fifty years ago. But she had fought her bishop to a standstill on several occasions. One was over the use of children in a morality play. The bishop wanted the children to act the vices as well as the virtues. But she thought it would do them damage to act such roles, so she entered a public dispute and got him to use adults. And that led to further judgments on her part about the church's use of people that would cause all kinds of confusion in those who wanted their saints clean of controversy. But what delicious poetry! John of the Cross couldn't do better. "Damn you, Beauty, if you fool us and we never come back as you do!"

The man who screened the candidates liked this woman, but saw she wouldn't make it past the first desk upstairs. So he decided to be tactful but explicit in his rejection letter to the lay group that had sent the material in. "Dear Committee: You submitted the portrait of a lovable woman to our office. We are grateful that you did so because it reminds us of how varied and beautiful the work of God's grace is. What we pick up as positive is the lifelong charity of your candidate. What we pick up as negative is her conflict with the church on several occasions. She was probably correct, so far as we can tell, but the climate here will not allow us to see struggling with church officials as a holy act. At one time it was, and there are great saints who fought popes, or bishops, or pastors. But these days, authority wants saints of obedience. We have read the poetry of your candidate very thoroughly and we think it is world class.

"We suggest you move toward making her known in the world of the arts first. As her influence spreads, her effect on people can be more clearly seen, particularly on religious people. That way her stature may emerge and draw people's attention to this life of charity you have submitted to us as cause for canonization. At that level political considerations will no longer prevent her case from being examined. At the moment the church cannot canonize attacks upon itself, as we noted earlier. We end with a quote to you from her own poetry, on the death of a missionary: 'The beauty of the earth knows the beauty it must bury.' Sincerely." And the man signed his name for the congregation and sent it back to the high valley of South America.

Within a few months there was a reply on his desk. The envelope was covered wtih stamps, because inflation was so great where the letter came from. He opened it and read: "Dear Congregation: Thank you for your judgment. But we had thought that, if people knew she was a saint, they would then read her poetry. You seem to think that if they read her poetry, the sanctity will be evident and declaration will be easier. You must see that we have no way out of this impasse except through you. Who will translate her otherwise, who will publish her, who will evaluate her life in terms of her art? So many great voices have disappeared. We fear that outcome for her. So we ask you to reconsider and see if you can't present her cause on a higher lever. Sincerely." And the group signed the letter.

The man knew they were right, it was harder to be a secular saint than it was to be a sacred one. And that didn't end the complication. He had on his desk the dossier of a young Jewish woman, a convert to the church, who was killed in one of the camps, and was now proposed as a martyr. But that meant there were six million martyrs, because she was really killed as a Jew, not a Christian. And there was a story in the paper about another victim who stayed Jewish but wrote a journal right up to the last minute celebrating the beauty of his life. World class holiness no Churchman would ever touch! The man now had a choice to respond officially and damage their hopes, or to respond personally and have them live apart from the church.

He wrote: "Dear Committee: Return the material to me. I will arrange to have her works translated into the several languages required by the committee members who do the scrutiny. But I will not submit her works to those committee members, because I know they will simply refuse to read them. However I will be sure the translations are done very well by people here who have a knowledge of poetry in their own tongues. I will then return the translated material to you for your own judgment. I will send copies to several publishing houses here in the city, implying in my letter that at some time in the future my office may be interested in her cause. Even though I know it won't. But who can tell?

"You are to do the same with publishers you contact in your region. My view is that we should try to make her known as a poet. And that may be more than what this office can offer. I visit many churches of many saints here and know or care to know very few of them since there is so much fiction involved, or situations that have no bearing on the present.

"I think the full value of your candidate can be felt without the church, if we succeed in getting her known as a poet. The sanctity of people is far too great and complex for our small church to handle. That is why we pick and choose, why we sometimes pick well, sometimes poorly. Our declarations can do harm as well as good. I would meantime ask you what you may have already asked of yourselves, to see all sanctity as the touch of the holy on and in the human soul. That way we can stay with what we have yet love what we have not and use it for our soul's good. I look forward to the return of the material. I can do some of the translation myself. Meantime I quote her to you again: 'I made this grave of loose rocks/and shaped them like a face/eager to know what comes next.'" He signed his own name and sent the letter off. When he returned to his desk, a new stack was waiting for him, the morning mail. He felt himself eager to begin.

39. Her Honor the Judge

For the Eleventh Sunday in Ordinary Time

I will not nullify the grace of God; if righteousness comes by law, then Christ died for nothing.

GALATIANS 2:21

There was a woman who was a judge in a Criminal court. The case before her this day was one of prostitution, involving a madam who ran an elegant, refined service for an elegant Brahmin-class clientèle. The evidence was so clear that the defense admitted guilt and looked to mitigating circumstances to lower the penalty, which could be ten years and a hundred thousand dollars.

The woman who was the judge sat looking at the woman who ran the prostitution ring. There was a pallor to the woman's beautiful skin, not from regret, but from some fear as to where ten years in jail would take her life. The madam knew what time would do to her body. She had never let anyone use it but herself, that was clear from what she admitted. She had made it a place that was untouchable, beautiful, precious to herself, because that way she could see how much people wanted her, or wanted what she could provide. Now people wanted to put her untouchable self in jail.

The woman judge was handsome in her own way. She was very tall. She had married an even taller man. When the family was together, husband, and their three children, they seemed like rare species, but they were easygoing and at home with the shorter world. The judge was relaxed now as she listened to the lawyers ask for the most each could get: full penalty, full fine; token penalty, token fine. There was media coverage. The madam was a photographer's gem, the story a gem for the yellow press. When the defense sat down, the judge let a silence settle on the court. She sat in her chair looking from one lawyer to the other, then at the defendant, then at the press, then at her notes in front of her.

"The law requires me to judge you guilty, since you have pleaded guilty to a violation of law."

As the judge spoke, the woman's lawyer nudged her to rise. She did. Her clothes were loose. There were only hints of the elegant form that they covered. She was modestly, richly dressed, so as to please, not titillate.

The judge said, "The law does not require me to give you a fixed sentence. It leaves it to my discretion to be harsh or lenient, and it leaves you an appeal if you think me harsh." The judge had brought herself face-to-face with this woman. "Tell me which I should be," she said.

The defense attorney interrupted and said, "Your honor, I speak for my client, and I think you should judge leniently."

The woman judge looked at the lawyer and said, "Your arguments were unconvincing. That's why I'm asking her. She has no obligation to respond."

The woman under judgment was silent.

"I'm going to sentence you to five years of public service and place you on probation for that five years," the judge said. "What can you do best?"

A laugh burst out in the courtroom. The irony was too much for the crowd. But the judge sat calmly and waited until the laughter died down. Silence grew as the woman said nothing in response.

"I want you to speak to me," said the judge.

"I can organize," said the woman.

"Could you organize the recovery of prostitutes?" the judge asked.

"If I had to," said the woman, "But I'd be dead before I got very far."

There was a cold, sober tone to her voice as she stated the cold, sober fact.

"I know that," said the judge. "I also know you're dead for what you already know, the names, the places. I'm trying to get a little good from you before someone finishes you off."

"Someone good?" said the woman.

"Probably," said the judge, "someone who wants to *stay* good."

The woman under judgment relaxed a bit; she moved the cuffs

of her long sleeves back so her fine wrists and hands showed more and the thin gold bracelets made a rattling sound.

The judge said, "I mean if you give a signal that names will stay confidential, and that people can come to you who want to move discreetly back on this side of the law?"

The woman put one hand up and laid it on her neck as if to feel herself swallow. Then she touched her hair, near her shoulder and let her hand drop to her side, again with the light rattle of bracelets.

"I mean the sentence is not really being passed in this courtroom," said the judge.

The woman's hands pressed in lightly against her thighs. She was not looking at the judge, she was looking at the base of the judge's bench. Her hands came up over her stomach and crossed at the waist where she held them, the two beautiful hands going in either direction.

The judge said, "You are pleading for leniency from people we don't know."

The woman raised her head, and moved it slightly to free her hair from her face.

"But if you are under probation from the court, and if you are dealing with people who want out, and if you are keeping their secrets, you may get a judgment of leniency from them as well as us."

As the judge spoke the woman grew paler; she became more attractive, the more vulnerable she became.

"Because too many people will know who and where you are for anyone to hit you," said the judge.

"It's a slim chance," said the woman.

"It's very slim," said the judge. "But it's there."

The woman was now perfectly still and looking at the judge eye to eye. She was not tense. Her clothing rested easily on her, half concealing, half revealing, but she was really in her body, feeling it, feeling maybe a future where there had not been one.

The judge said, "I would have you work for a recovery group that has no relation to the law, one that keeps its secrets and is known as such."

"Will they take me?"

"If you want to do their work."

There was a long, long pause, the woman uncrossed her hands, reached up to lift her blouse a bit by the shoulders and let it fall into a careless shape again, which increased her charm, as she wondered whether she could cross a certain line. She then looked at the judge as a whole new idea dawned on her. "You're trying to save me," she said.

"No, I'm not. I'm trying to make sense of what I see before me, since your lawyer did not."

The woman seemed relieved. She looked at the judge, saw her tall body, tall even when seated, saw the fine cheekbones, the gray-black hair, the steady look, the hands folded with the wide gold band showing. She was looking at a woman who was looking at her as a woman. "I can do their work," she said.

"Then that is what I sentence you to," said the judge. "And I require of you a ten thousand dollar fine. And I suggest to you that whatever wealth you have you give away irrevocably to charity. This will not fool anyone who is judging you apart from this court. But it will influence the court. That other court will only be influenced if it knows it does not have to silence you."

The woman took a step back as the judge said those words. Yet her step was firm.

"Agreed," she said.

There was a kind of surprised murmur in the court that a defendant should speak that way to a sentencing judge, but it was exactly what the judge wanted and it showed on her face. She said, "I will hold you briefly in custody until the recovery agency can be contacted. I will appoint the group as your probation officer. I will keep in constant touch with them, but not with you. This court respects their secrecy. This court hopes that will protect you and provide you with reform. Court is adjourned."

The bailiff announced, "The court will rise!" Everyone did, but no one moved for a few minutes. The drama had gone. No one could think where.

40. A Monument to the Dead

For the Twelfth Sunday in Ordinary Time

On that day a fountain shall be opened for the line of David and for the inhabitants of Jerusalem, to remove all sin and impurity.

ZECHARIAH 13:1

A man was passing a monument to the dead on his way to a museum. Business trip. Foreign city. One of the great museums in the world. The monument was to men dead in a civil war, so far as he could tell. The monument was an ugly thing—a drooping Athena at the top and three water steps down to either side like stiles over an English hedgerow. Then a bathtub spilling water into a square with small rocks of varied colors at the bottom. Chiseled below Athena were the words: "Glory. Honor. Eternal Memory. For Those Who Died for Their Country." Heavy, heavy words, for dead everyone had forgotten by now, for it was fifty years back to that civil war.

The man kept going. He remembered a First World War veteran he had known, a *poilu*, who had become a priest after it by special permission. He had lost both legs in a grenade-tossing duel with German soldiers. They were on either side of a farmyard wall, early in the war, before both sides dug trenches and paid a hundred thousand lives for every thousand yards' advance. "We were fools," the old soldier used to say. "We fought like fools, and we paid the price of fools." He was in his nineties when he died. He was glad to go, old age hurt him so much.

The businessman came to a light and a crossing over the wide boulevard. He noticed a man with Down's syndrome on the other side of the street. The man was perfectly disciplined, looking at the light, looking at the pedestrian lane, the light, the lane. Other people simply crossed when there was no traffic. The businessman had never been in a war. His body was perfectly developed.

His legs were under him. He would have no monument for that. Nor would women, who mainly didn't die in wars. They died by other violences.

He came to the great museum, went in and simply followed his own leanings. There were some fine Crucifixions in the first hall—the Greek-god body of Jesus in all kinds of torment and glory. Then there were some marvelous Virgin Mothers, mostly of the fat Flemish kind with a breast out in case the babe or the mystics watching got hungry. One Virgin Mother was squirting milk from one breast in a perfect arc into the mouth of Saint Bernard, who was in ecstasy. In another room he saw a painting of a goddess spurting out the Milky Way. Both women were good shots. "That's the kind of war to be in," he thought. Then he came to a Judith and Holofernes. Then he came to another. Then to a third: Judith with a scimitar, a maid near her holding the bag that would hold the head. And the great body of Holofernes with his head still on, mighty, curly, asleep, drunk. In fact he saw five paintings of Judith and Holofernes. Then a few of David and Goliath. Then a few of Saint Sebastian with arrows sticking through him every which way. And there was a picture of another saint holding the saw that had sawn her in two. Then he saw the mighty battle at the wedding feast between the Lapiths and the Centaurs. And lastly there was a marvelous Salome dancing with a dish with the Baptist's head. The whole museum was a monument to murder and murderers. Maybe the whole Bible too. The man felt a fierce desire to find something that wasn't. So he left through a turnstile that clacked like an empty machine gun.

He walked back along the tree-lined boulevard to the Plaza Colon, where there was a mighty set of stones above a pool glorifying and honoring the discoverer of the New World, names of crew, of chaplains, of places, and quotes, one of which said they had discovered an earthly paradise. The man knew they had made an earthly hell of that paradise, wiping out the whole population within forty years. Yet these great jagged hunks of stone seemed to say some mighty creation had taken place. As he took the underground passage to the other side of the street, he saw a woman wrapped in burlap, smoking a cigarette, seated against the wall and staring at the ceiling. Then out on the sidewalk again there was a beggar who rattled his pan at a woman walking by with her dog, then made a pass with his free hand to get a touch of the wooly coat, missed, smiled, then went dead serious and needy as he waved at the next person who passed by.

As the man came to the entrance to his hotel, a three-wheeled motorized chair pulled in front of him and stopped. The driver seemed to pitch head first toward the concrete, but at the last second put two hands out as fists that hit like bowling balls, then his legless trunk swung like a pendulum to a perfect landing beneath him, and he moved like a stork into a doorway and through.

"Life is whatever you land on, or whatever lands on you," the man thought. And in his mind he saw again the picture of Saint Bernard in ecstacy, with his mouth open and the Virgin's squirt of milk landing perfectly on his tongue. And then he saw the Baptist's purple head, eyes closed, unable to see the bare, beautiful arms that held him aloft, the head turned, the fierce flame in the cheeks as Salome danced him toward her mother, who had her dress ripped open in ululation.

"That's it!" the man thought. "I'll put up a monument to the dead. It'll be Salome, not Athena. And there will be ping pong balls spilling out of the dish she dances over her head. The balls will have faces painted on them. And everyone killed will have a real photo of himself pasted on a ping pong ball, an I.D. photo, and the balls will bounce crazily down the back and shoulders and breasts of Salome, caroming at all angles down stairs into a square pool that will seethe with them before they are sucked down a hole, then back up to spill out of the dish again. And anyone who knows someone dead can go and see him come out of the dish, bounce like a fool for a while, then start the trip again.

Or maybe I should just put Holofernes up there without his head and have all the ping pong balls pouring out of his severed neck. Or maybe Judith as she swings the sack up over her shoulder and goes back through the lines. The cross is whatever head we carry. Doesn't matter whose," he thought.

He went into his hotel, to the bar, and surprised the barman with an order for milk. Then he looked at the glass in front of him and said, "Do something, please!" It didn't. So he surprised the barman with an order for scotch, poured it in the milk and drank it.

"I have to make things happen for myself," he thought. "Wish I didn't."

41. Lot's Wife Wins One

For the Thirteenth Sunday in Ordinary Time

But if you are led by the Spirit, you are not under law.

GALATIANS 5:18

Lot and Lot's wife were packing to leave Sodom.

She said to him, "What's with this sudden move? You owe someone some money?"

"Do what I say. I'll explain later!"

"Explain what later? There's desert out there, that's where people get lost and die!"

"We won't get lost, we won't die!" he said. "Now pack, will you? Before it's too late!"

"Shall I bring your ceremonial robes? They're really heavy," she said.

"No, leave them."

"You don't look so good in burlap."

"Will you stop fooling around!"

"I'm not fooling," she said, "Look, I'm naked and ready, no clothes, no hairpins, nothing but a smile!"

"If people saw you naked they'd pull you to pieces," he said.

"Then how about this sack," she said, "with a rope around the middle. I could wear a veil and look like a walking tree with a chirping bird inside."

"Yes," he said, "that's fine, but no chirping, we have to look normal."

"Normal," she said, " a bunch of people with a bag apiece walking out into the desert, in the noonday sun, cuckoo, that's what it is, cuckoo! You better tell me what's up, or I'll draw a crowd!"

"Look," he said, "this place is going to get destroyed by fire and brimstone, any minute now, as soon as we get out of here."

"Who says?"

"God."

"What God?"

"God, God, there's only one," he said, "and he told me to get out of here, he's going to wipe this place out!"

"For what?" she said, "For what?"

"For wickedness," he said, "for total, absolute, utter wickedness."

"God's as bad as they are if he does it."

"I'm in no position to argue."

"Well, I am."

"Later," he said, "when we're out of here."

"There is no out of here," she said, "If god can be merciless here, God can be merciless there, like that desert sun that kills everything green and bleaches our skulls white."

"I cannot speak for God."

"But you've been talking to him."

"No, he talks, I listen."

"You listen?" she said, "you listen to him tell you he's going to wipe this place out with fire and brimstone?"

"It's a wicked place."

"But," she said, "if you wipe out a wicked place you become a wicked place yourself, don't you understand? Doesn't he? Where is he? Bring me? He's got to hear! Let go of me!"

"I'm not letting go of you," he said, "If I have to carry you out of here like a rug, I'll do it!"

"Where is he?" she said, "up there, behind the sun, blinding me! Out there, in the hot sand, sucking me dry? In the black night freezing me to death? Is he in you? Look at you shaking in fear! Is he the fear and shaking in you?"

"What do you want me to do?"

"Tell him to stop," she said, "He'll end up as wicked as they are, hurling fire and brimstone from the sky like a kid throwing rocks at a nest of eggs!"

"Okay," he said, "I'll tell him, I'll tell him! Now grab that skin of water and let's go!"

"Grab nothing," she said, "tell him now!"

"He's not here."

"I guess not!" she said, "it's too dangerous here. Tell him to come here, tell him to stand under fire and brimstone and feel it on his flesh and blood, children's flesh and blood, animals' flesh and blood, trees' flesh and blood!"

"We have to go, we have to go," he said.

"Why?"

"Because if we don't there will be nothing left of anyone anywhere."

"Then stay," she said, "and he won't dare destroy this place!"

"Well, I can't leave without you!"

"Why not?"

"Oh, what a thing to ask me," he said, "you know I'm dead when you are, I'm alive when you are! If you stay, I stay!"

"You know," she said, "if you stay he will not destroy this place with fire and brimstone! He'll have to come himself!"

"I know it now," he said.

"And what if I stayed here alone," she said, "would he stop for me?"

"Yes."

"And what about the wicked?" she said.

"They'll never know!" he said.

42. Biodegradable Bombardier

For the Fourteenth Sunday in Ordinary Time

> This you shall see and be glad at
>   heart,
> your limbs shall be as fresh as
>   grass in spring;
> the Lord shall make his power
>   known among his servants
> and his indignation felt among
>   his foes.
>
> Isaiah 66:14

There was a man who wanted to purge the world. So badly it made him laugh at his own foolishness. He was nonviolent now, so he would have to use a world-size dose of milk of magnesia or shampoo or Fels Naptha. He had loved that strange brand name when he was young and sent to the store to buy some, just as he had loved Arm & Hammer soda and paregoric and epsom salts for their magical names and properties. He had had a nail in his foot when he was six and had to put it in hot linseed packs to draw the poison. Imagine a hot linseed pack on the wicked world. But the lies were thick in these later years of his life. And they came hard on the heels of the racism of his middle years and the war of his early years, and he had all he could do to keep himself from muttering, "I'm a Dead Sea and the crap floats, the crap of a lifetime."

He had said it out loud once. A friend was walking by and said hello, so the man knew the friend had heard. It was embarrassing. And he couldn't purge himself by confessing. Confessing! He went to a priest once in the box and told the priest he had committed one sin of war and two sins of sex. The priest asked him about the sex, realized it wasn't unnatural, with sheep or something subhuman, then let him go with a scolding about treating women as things and gave him ten minutes of prayer. But not a question about the war, his toggling bombs off on defenseless enemy cities.

No one lived through those firestorms. He could see them through the nose cone when he came in on the last wave. That was purging, under orders, and nothing was purged. Sodom and Gomorrah has metastasized.

"Damn, I shouldn't use disease," he thought. He had seen another friend the day before, eaten alive with cancer and ready to go whenever the thing wished.

"The good get purged," he said, and a girl a table away looked at him. No, not a girl, a young woman. This coffee shop was right for everyone. And he was an old man with scars three ways on his face, from shrapnel, there were guns still able in that fire-bombed city.

"I'm losing my marbles," he said across to her. His voice was hoarse, from smoking, but he didn't smoke any more.

"You sure you had some to lose?" she said.

"I'm not sure. Come give me an IQ test. I can't finish this bran muffin, and there's some butter."

She moved her cup and books over to his table and sat looking at him with a very scientific look. "I'm in geriatric nursing," she said, "I'll get my degree next year."

"You must be crazy," he said. "You never throw something new at something old. I've seen whole forests burned so seedlings can have a chance."

"You just failed my first test," she said.

So he looked at her. "I haven't been this close to a young life in a long time," he said. "I feel like a wizened apple."

"What's 'wizened' mean?"

"Wrinkled."

"Then you should say 'wrinkled.'"

"But I was trying to make a pun," he said.

She looked puzzled.

"Well, I meant 'wrinkled' also means 'wisened up.' So 'wizened' means both at the same time, you get it?"

"I'm afraid so," she said. "Tell me why you think you're losing your marbles."

"Well, I want a clean world again before I leave it. I started out clean. I mean I crapped things up like everybody else, but that was physical and didn't stick. Babies' skins are miracles. And women's breasts sometimes. But I'm not finishing up clean. And it's moral. And it sticks. I want to clean everything else up with myself. And I know there's something out there fresh and clean as a baby, or a woman, but you can't touch it unless you're like it, and look at me!"

"You are kind of beat up," she said.

He laughed at that and loved it. It made him feel like the old wrangler who could still bust steers.

"But you can't go back," she said. "Just as I can't go forward."

"Don't want to go back," he said. "I want to go clean."

"Maybe this is the way you get cleaned."

"Like I'm biodegradable?"

"Yes."

"That's a thought. I just follow the croaking and I come out clean. Down through drool and stool to a stiff in a box. I guess I wanted a lightning flash and a scar on a tree trunk to mark it."

"Some people walk out when they can," she said.

"Not me." That idea still stunned him. "You know some?" he asked.

"Yes," she said. "There's always a note on the suicidal ones' charts. And you have to keep an eye on their relatives too."

"Would you stop them?"

"Yes, I would."

"Then what would you tell them? 'Be good or I'll lick you'?"

"You're trying to hurt me," she said. "Maybe your purging is really an attempt to hurt. Maybe you don't want to go to that bosom in the sky. It's the bosom here you want."

"It does seem like that. I'm sorry if it does. But it isn't. I want to go. But I want a chance to leave something fresh behind. Not a bad smell when the elevator door opens and no one is inside. And it can't be physical. So it's got to be moral and I can't think!"

"Let me finish that muffin," she said. "It's too good to leave."

"Sure," he said, "and the butter. Maybe if I just croak with good grace. Instead of like that guy in the movie who said *'Horror!'* just before."

"You think it's been a horror?" she asked.

"Well, no," he said. "There have been horrors, but no, there's the beauty. And you're sitting there young. And I can still eat butter and not have a heart attack."

"So maybe the last word does it," she said. "Maybe you have to practice for the last word you want to say."

He just looked at her, and a laugh of relief burst out of him. "Right," he said, "right."

Then he just looked at her and flushed with a kind of love, a kind of thanks. He put out his hand, and she shook it. He got up and squared himself, still grinning, zipped his jacket, put out his hand again, and she shook it again. "I'll see you," he said. "Yes," she said.

43. "No," She Said.

For the Fifteenth Sunday in Ordinary Time

> It is a thing very near to you, upon your lips and in your heart ready to be kept.
>
> DEUTERONOMY 30:14

A woman was waiting one day in a New York subway. She was far uptown and needed to get down to Penn Station to take Amtrak to Boston. It was a hot day, and a crowded subway. The A train was just squealing into the station when she saw a man pitch headlong from the crowd onto the tracks, and she saw another man dart back through the crowd toward the turnstiles and the stairs up. The motorman hit the brakes and the cars made a wild moan to stop but went over the man nonetheless and halted halfway into the station. The woman raced toward a fire alarm box away from the train, pulled the alarm, then raced back to the train where the crowd was in a panic. No one but the motorman dared go down in the pit with the live rail so close. He shouted up that the man underneath was still alive and someone should call the police and the fire department. The woman had already done this, so she stood teetering at the platform edge, hoping against hope that the man was okay.

It would take time for help to come. The crowd got calmer. Some people went out to get a bus. And word began to spread that someone had pushed someone in front of a train. The woman remembered the racing figure, and a feeling of outrage rose in her throat, but she stopped any words from coming, and she waited as the voices flew all around her. Then the emergency squads came clanking in with enough equipment for the whole crowd. The live rail was turned off, and the medics went over the edge of the platform and down under the train. Soon everyone could hear the firm, taut voices of the experts, and everyone thought they could hear the feeble voice of the victim.

The woman saw there was nothing she could do; she would miss her Boston train if she stayed longer. So she went to a policeman and said: "I think I saw what happened. I saw the man go onto the tracks and someone escape through the crowd."

The policeman said, "Did you see him being pushed?"

"No," the woman said.

"Well, did you get a make on the man who beat it?"

"No, not really," she said, "I just saw movement."

"Thanks," the policeman said, "but we really need hard facts."

"Well, do you want my name?" she asked.

"No, lady," he said, "it won't do any good."

"Will the man be all right?"

"Can't tell," he said, "Read the *Times* in the morning."

The women left through the turnstile she had seen the criminal use, and went up the same stairs as he, and she looked for a cab to take her to Penn Station. There were many people trying to do the same thing. The power was still out in the subway. Her outrage had turned into real pity for things. There was a kind of grief coming out through the pores of her skin. This must have caught a cabbie's eye because a cab pulled up besider her. She said through the window, "Penn Station?" as a question, and the cabbie said, "Sure, get in." She got in, the cabbie flicked the meter, cut into traffic, and headed downtown.

"You been hurt?" he asked.

"Yes," she said, "I just saw someone pushed under a train."

"Another one!" said the cabbie, and hit the wheel with his fist. "Man or woman?"

"Man," the woman said. "And still alive. I think I could hear him."

"You want me to get you some aspirin?" the cabbie said.

"No. Thanks." she said. "Just make some sense out of this."

"Oh," he said, "that'd hurt you more. Maybe the guy underneath is a pusher too, in his own way, maybe a pimp someone's sore at, maybe he's foolin' with someone's girl. Or maybe he teaches Sunday school, I don't know."

"But you wouldn't want it to happen to him like this, would you?" she said.

"No," he said, "no, never. A lot of my friends would. But me, no. I saw my own kids born, and I buried my parents, and that's the way life is for me, you don't burn anybody in between. Though you have to duck a lot of shit. You got kids?"

"No," she said. "But I will soon. It's time. Though I don't know what I'm bringing them into."

"Well," the cabbie said, "you're bringin' 'em into you, and you sound like enough to me."

"Well," she said, "I might be a pusher too, or a madam, or I might have stolen someone else's man!"

"No, lady, you smell different," the cabbie said. "You felt that, what happened. The others don't feel."

"I wish I didn't feel," she said. "I have these two images, a guy getting pushed, a guy running away. The cop told me to look in the *New York Times* for what happens next."

"Naw," the cabbie said, "don't. You know what happened next. You felt it. Somebody else didn't. They'll do all they can to help the guy underneath. The other guy's long gone. Keep feeling it, and guys like me will keep giving you cheap advice. I saw you there, and I knew you were real. So I know I'm not dead. Meter says six bucks and sign says Penn Station. This entrance okay?"

"Why don't you just drive me to Boston," she said. "It's a bad world outside this cab."

"My wife would kill me," he said. "I mean she wouldn't like it. But she'd like you. I mean I think she would. So take care!"

"Goodbye," the woman said. She got out and went into the station. They were loading the Boston train so she went to the platform. She stopped for a moment before entering the car. To her left were empty platforms and pits where people could fall or be pushed.

"No," she said, "no, no." And she entered her train.

44. Man Hunt

For the Sixteenth Sunday in Ordinary Time

—to make known how rich and glorious it is among all nations. The secret is this: Christ in you, the hope of a glory to come.

COLOSSIANS 1:27

There was a man who was too busy to think. He knew it the day he patted his wife on the head at the breakfast table and called her Rex. During the day he sold stocks, phones on either shoulder and hands on a computer. Sometimes his secretary would put half a sandwich in his mouth for lunch. It muffled his speech, but he still bought and sold stocks.

One evening he said to his wife and two daughters, "I'm too busy to think. So I want in the evenings to go for a long walk alone in the park and maybe remember who I am."

His wife was silent, but his twelve-year-old daughter said, "Let me go too. I love that park, and she won't let me go out alone."

"Who's 'she'?" the man asked.

"You know. *Her*," the daughter said, looking toward her mother.

The eight-year-old slumped in her chair like a little thunder storm. "She gives *her* everything," she said. "She'll let her go with you and keep me to wipe the damn dishes."

"What's with this 'damn'?" the man said.

"Well, you listen if I say it," the younger child said. "I want to go too. There are chipmunks in the walls and they scoot in one hole and come out another, you never know where."

"To hell with the damn dishes," his wife said. "We'll all go for a walk in the park and find out who we are. Though this is a good enough show for anyone to find out."

"Look," the man said, "I just want to go meditate in the park. Just quiet myself down and see if I'm still one and not a million spare parts in a garage somewhere. Just let the trees and the chip-munks and the stone walls get inside me instead of crazy voices shouting 'buy' or 'sell' or 'hold' or a lot of other damn nonsense."

"See, you said it too," muttered the younger child. "It's okay for you."

"Well, I'm a big dog," the man said, "and big dogs can go 'damn, damn.'"

"And that makes me a kitty," the eight-year-old said. "I have to go 'meow, meow.' She just wants me to dry up and blow away."

"Oh," the wife said, "I make you eat the right things, so I'm Ebenezer Scrooge."

"He's a man," the child said. "Okay for a man to be mean."

"This is not going right," the man said, "Nobody knows who anybody is. I'll stay home and do the damn dishes, and you all go for a walk in the park."

"No," said the twelve-year-old, "I want to go with you. I'll keep my mouth shut, unlike some people I know."

"Oh," said the wife, "why don't the three of you go, and I'll do the damn dishes. I've done them so often they tell me things about my life. But not if you're around."

"What do they tell you?" asked the older girl.

"Oh, they tell me my husband is a telephone with a nice kiss and a firm goodbye. And my elder daughter doesn't want to use my name because it cramps her style, and my younger daughter doesn't want to use my name because that keeps me off her back. Things like that."

"Dumb dishes," said the eight-year-old.

"What are you guys up to?" the man said, "This is like a hockey game with a lot of slap shots. I thought you liked each other."

"We do," the wife said, "but it's like having too many daisies in the same pot. They choke each other. That's why we all want to go on that walk with you. I like the oaks, they're big and they groan in the wind, great spooky stuff even on clear nights."

"Yeah, but they're old," the older girl said. "Old and wrinkled, and they conk you on the head with acorns in the fall."

"That's good for the chipmunks," the child said. "They put them in their cheeks and sometimes can't get into their holes in the wall, and it's funny as hell watching them make up their minds to spit one out, they just don't want to, and they go 'chrrr chrrr' they're so mad, and they spin like break dancers to have it both ways and they can't . . ."

"Whoa," said the man, "whoa! You don't need to go to the park. You have it all in your head."

"But I don't have you," the eight-year-old said.

"And I don't either," the wife said, "but I don't mean that as a crack. I think we all lose one another after a while. Then nobody admits anything. I think I like that park in the winter best. Everything is bare and you can see the shapes of the earth and the rare, soft colors of the winter sky."

"But there are no chipmunks," the child said, "just some ratty gray squirrels."

"They're not ratty," the wife said, "their fur is plump and perfect for the cold."

"I like the crows in the winter," the older girl said. "They're so black and floppy. They caw at each other like crazy, and they fly like you threw a dishrag at someone."

"That's hitting too close to home," the man said. "Look, you all know that park, and what you like, and I don't. I just want to walk there and listen to myself."

"I told you I won't say a word," the older girl said. "You won't even know I'm there."

"And you won't know that I'm there either," said the child. "I'll play with the chipmunks. Maybe I'll find a hole in the wall big enough for me. I'll fill it up with acorns and you won't ever see me again."

"And what about you?" said the man to his wife.

"Oh," she said, "I'm proud. I need to be asked."

"Then please come," the man said.

"To mind the kids?" she asked.

"No," he said, "to mind me. I've got a daughter who wants to be a chipmunk, and a daughter who wants to be a crow, and a wife who wants to be a winter you can see the colors of the sky through. I may want to turn into something myself, a ratty squirrel, and that'd be murder over the phone to people who want to buy and sell. No, you come and mind me," he said, "or I'll turn into something screwy." ·

"Like a phone," she said, "that kisses and says a firm goodbye."

"Yes."

"I knew it," the eight-year-old said, "she's back to those damn dishes."

45. Chips Off the Old Block

For the Seventeenth Sunday in Ordinary Time

> Abraham replied, "May I presume to speak to the Lord, dust and ashes that I am: suppose there are five short of the fifty good men? Wilt thou destroy the whole city for a mere five men?" He said, "If I find forty-five there I will not destroy it."
>
> GENESIS 18:27–28

There was a man who stopped praying because prayer made nothing happen. But after a while he felt very lonely. The same things were going on, but now he was alone with them, and he was worse off than before. So he joined some liberal groups.

"I won't be alone this way," he thought. But his liberal groups lost cause after cause, and the man was more alone than before. So he joined some conservative groups. And they won cause after cause. But that intensified the man's loneliness because no one ever listened. They just spoke and spoke and did and did. There was no yesterday and no tomorrow.

The man turned to his women friends, but they were afraid of him. He was too empty and might swallow them whole. He turned to his men friends, but they thought him too emotional and unable to fit in. And he was more alone than before.

"Maybe alone is good," he said. But it wasn't. So he went back to prayer and said, "God, you make nothing happen."

"Right," said God.

"Then what's with this praying," the man said. "There is more war and more disaster now than I've ever read about. And we could blow this thing up in your face."

"Right," said God, "in my face. What's left of it. Silly pun, no?"

"You Spanish?" the man asked.

"Some days yes," God said. "Why?"

"I don't know why," the man said. "Someone said the other day that to be God is to be a rich man in Spain."

"Wrong," said God. "Wrong. It's to be a poor man in Spain and thumbing a ride on a donkey."

"But you make donkeys."

"Right. But they have a mind of their own. I make a lot of things. But once made, they have minds of their own. The rhinoceros. The mule."

"This all sounds so silly."

"It is," God said. "So say something serious."

"I can't. It hurts too much. I feel like telling you a dirty joke: A white horse fell in the mud."

"Give me a minute to get over that."

"You seem to get over everything. Years after year you get over everything."

"That hurt," God said. "You know I don't. Did you ever have your eyes dilated? You can't keep the light out—you see everything too much, and you can't leave the doctor's office. Okay, suppose your eyes don't close and you have to leave the doctor's office. And thumb a ride on a donkey."

"You're being very nice to me," the man said. "But I'm more than five years old. You don't have to be like an ad on TV."

"I know, but I'm very tired today. You're the first one I've talked to. And I thought I'd horse around a bit. Take some pressure off. So okay, what do you want, metaphysics? Rock 'em, sock 'em theology?"

"No," the man said, "no. I've been that route. It's like eating a newspaper for breakfast. Just tell me why nothing happens when you're around. I mean things just go on whether you're here or not."

"I told you things have a mind of their own. I don't have a big board and push buttons. I have a big headache and Anacin isn't enough."

"Tell me."

"Oh, I could," God said. "Then you'd have a headache and you'd walk out and I'd spend the rest of the time talking to myself. Somebody would think I was crazy."

"Give it to me a little at a time. Maybe I'm not such a patsy."

"Okay, just take the lies. Somebody says I'm like such and such, and I'm going to kill anyone who's not. Then somebody says I'm not like that at all, and I'm going to kill whoever says I am. Then somebody says I stoke fires in hell, and somebody says I spray perfume in heaven, and somebody says I'm a heartless bastard, and somebody says I'm soft on crime. Do you see? And you say I'm a mover and shaker who just sits there with a toothpick in his or her mouth letting things happen when I could stop them."

"Well, are you a man or a woman?"

"Give me a piece of cheese," God said, "I'm a mouse. That makes us even for the white horse and the mud."

"I really mean that question. If you're a man, you'll think I'm too emotional. Not able to fit in. If you're a woman, you'll think I'm empty and want to gobble you up. Just like the people here."

"I'm not that kind of man," God said, "nor that kind of woman. Emotion is all I have left. What did I just tell you? And go ahead gobble me up. It'll take you time. And there's no Anacin for it."

"You're right," the man said. "One would have to be crazy to be God. And this is the craziest conversation I've ever been in."

"You have to be crazy to be human, too," God said. "And this is *not* the craziest conversation I've ever been in. This is fun. You should hear what I hear when a holy war is going on. Or when someone's in a crap game at Las Vegas and their whole life is on the table."

"What happens when there are disasters, when people figure you won't do anything?"

"There is silence," God said. "And I'm left alone with the whole burden of what has happened. Until someone like you comes along who is willing to listen. I can take it, but I hate to take it alone."

"Why?"

"You tell me."

"You fall in the mud alone," the man said.

"Right," God said. "Right."

46. Leading a Dog's Life

For the Eighteenth Sunday in Ordinary Time

> Stop lying to one another, now that you have discarded the old nature with its deeds and have put on the new nature, which is being constantly renewed in the image of its Creator and brought to know God.
>
> COLOSSIANS 3:9–10

A man was out walking his dog one day, along a fine old street. The dog was an Airedale. He named it Airedale because the name sounded so lyrical for such a wire-haired mutt. Airedale scared up some rats under a juniper bush, and they vanished down a hole just ahead of his nose.

"Damn!" said the man, "what brings rats? Birdseed!" He looked up and saw a bird feeder hanging from a tree and on it a whole gang of finches feeding on thistle seed. They were in their winter gray with black wings, and they were flapping at each other for a perch. For every seed they ate they dropped two.

"Nice," the man said, and forgot the rats and dog.

But then Airedale took off after a squirrel, went right between some trash barrels, knocked both over, and sped to the foot of a tree in which the squirrel sat jabbering down at him.

"What a mess!" the man said as he put the trash back in the barrels—scotch bottles, tomato juice bottles, beer bottles, they go in one barrel, papers in the other. He saw a photo of the massacre at the Rome airport in a newspaper that wrapped up some wet garbage, potato peelings and stuff. He said "Damn!" again, and grief took hold of him. He just stopped where he was, squatting down as if there was nothing left to live for. But Airedale snuffled under his arm after the potato peels wrapped up in the photo of the massacre, so the man said, "Git!" and set the barrels straight, the one clinking, the other rustling.

Then he followed Airedale, who was snuffling again, but this time on the trail of other dogs, from front stoops, to hydrants, to trees. Then there was a snarl, then two snarls, then one mighty snarl as two dogs had it out. The man ran and broke it up with his walking stick, grabbed Airedale by the collar and walked away stooped over like a pack animal trying to hold Airedale, who was going in six directions at once.

"It isn't worth it," he said as he put on the leash. "Everything's a dogfight. Even those finches were battling each other. And here I've got a stick that would kill King Kong. Someone opened fire on that crowd, people in a ticket line. It's as if those terrorists were masturbating with those guns!" Airedale pulled him toward a skunk hole. The man yanked him back. Airedale pulled him toward a crouched and hissing cat.

The man yanked him back. "Who's got a leash on me? Who's got a leash on anyone? You have to plead with people, 'Don't Shoot!' " He said that out loud, and someone walking by looked at him.

There was the Church of the Redeemmer with its Gothic tower and glorious copper beech tree. Mass was letting out.

"Don't shoot!" he said to himself as he tried to walk with dignity through the people with Airedale straining the leash ahead. Someone reached down and patted the dog and Airedale wanted to go away with her forever.

Someone spoke to the man, and he said, "Yes, Airedales are very good with children."

And he said, "Yes, great weather for winter."

And he said, "Yes, he really has me on the leash."

And "Yes, a great sermon."

But to himself. "You just have to walk a dog and the whole world is laid bare. I'm so happy and so sad I could burst either way." Then Airedale pulled free and ran and peed on the corner of the Church of the Redeemer to mark his territory, and came racing back with the leash in his mouth.

"Yes, a great sermon," the man said to himself. "If things were just ridiculous it'd be fine. I'll go in and make a visit in reparation, tie this beast to the handrail for a minute. No one will know we're Roman Catholics."

He went in and prayed: "Oh God, we are more dog than devil. We need someone to walk us, not wipe us out. There is a joy in everything. And there is a snarl. But love can change the snarl. Will you be with us and do so!" There was a snuffle at his elbow as Airedale tried to get into the pew and lick his face. The leash had come loose.

"They'll know we're Roman Catholics," the man said, and pulled Airedale after him out the door, past a few curious worshippers, and onto the sidewalk that led back home. "The only home I have is in joy and pain," the man said. Airedale trotted happily beside him on the leash, now undistracted by anything.

"I'm God," the man said, "I'm God!"

47. Guerrilla Gods

For the Nineteenth Sunday in Ordinary Time

For thou didst use the same means to punish our enemies and to make us glorious when we heard thy call.

WISDOM 18:8

"You forgive them when they're dead," the freedom fighter said to a reporter who was crouched with him in a stairwell near a window that looked right down a ruined street.

The question had been, "Can't you forgive and forget? There's nothing left here anyone would want."

Some shots began to ping through the hole that was the window; bits of mortar stung them on the cheeks.

The fighter said, "Quick, down stairs!" So they took the stairs two at a time and raced away from the stairwell as the rifle grenade came in and blew part of the stairway out.

"Wait here," said the fighter, and he went back over the rubble like a stork in rapid motion to the doorway under the blown-out window. He let loose a burst of fire straight down the street at the group shooting against him, caught one of them out in the open firing another rifle grenade, and took his knee off so the grenade went wild. It landed in an abandoned apartment and blew dishes and chairs out into the street already full of debris.

Back at the rear of the house the fighter said, "Now come, I tell you more."

That was the agreement—no cameras, just words. On the move. Take all the risks. Out the back door they went, moving parallel to the apartments to the street where the shots had come from, looking for another sniper point. They dodged into a building, up the back stairs, along a corridor, to a front apartment. Funny smell.

"Oh God," said the fighter, as he saw a dead baby up against a wall, "Must be a woman here too."

He pulled an upended table away, saw the swollen legs of the woman, dropped the table, and did a quick scout into what had been the kitchen. "Come," he said to the reporter.

He pointed to an old man and an old woman lying in the ruins of the kitchen. The fighter got on his small two-way radio, located himself, said what was in the apartment, signed off.

"So, forgive and forget?" said the fighter, "Yes, when they're dead!"

The reporter was a little sick from the smell. "Why don't you shoot from the corridor?"

The fighter laughed. "You want to be comfortable? That's funny. Okay. Doesn't matter. You ask more questions."

They went out into the corridor and found a window sniper's perch. The fighter crouched and looked down the street to see what moved.

"Ask," he said.

"Won't you all end up dead?"

"No, we won't. They will."

"How do you know this?"

"God," said the fighter.

"They have God too," said the reporter.

"No, there's only one. Ours."

There were some sounds behind them on the stairs. About five young men with body bags. After a quick exchange of words, the five disappeared inside. There was the noise of rubble being moved. Then in pairs they carted out the dead people in the apartment, old man with the baby, down the stairs and out the back, grunting as they went. The reporter heard a pickup truck pull away in the alley.

Then the five came back with weapons and spread upstairs to other vantage points. "We have just a short time. They will put in shells."

"Your god forgives," said the reporter.

"Not them," said the fighter. "He kills them first. Then he forgives."

"Why?" the reporter asked.

"You saw," said the fighter, "You want to see more? Come look! But move your head slowly. Like you didn't move it."

The reporter turned slowly, as if he weren't moving at all.

"Two houses down, second floor balcony. You see the more bodies? Even the dog?"

The reporter did.

"We cannot get them. They say come. We start. They shoot and kill us coming."

"It looks like a graveyard anyway," said the reporter.

"Okay, get ready," said the fighter. He popped up in the window and started to shoot down the street toward the entrance to a small supermarket. There was concentrated fire from upstairs also. After about five minutes, the reporter heard hard running down the stairs.

The fighter grabbed him by the sleeve and said, "Run!"

As they did, answering fire came slicing up from the small supermarket, and just as they reached the back door several artillery rounds hit the building, shaking it like a mop and sending chunks of concrete flying out windows over their heads. They all leaped into buildings on either side, went to the front and delivered a surprise fire down the street catching their opposites out in the open and bloodying them.

"This can go on forever," said the reporter, who had hardly enough breath to say it.

"You see us win," said the fighter, "Come," and they raced back out into the alley, then back up the stairs of the previously blasted building, this time to the roof from which they could see everything from behind the jagged remnants of it. "Now watch second and third floor across the street."

The reporter and the fighters were panting and sweating from the tremendous exertion of moving so fast. Fire opened from across the street from exactly where the fighter had said to look. And the group on the roof opened up on them immediately.

"You see they are stupid," said the fighter.

Just then the artillery rounds came back on the building. The reporter hugged a chimney from behind as terrific concussions tore the roof up around him. He saw his fighter actually flying through the air off the back edge of the roof as dead as anything the reporter had seen that day. He had been running for the back fire escape. The others had jumped down through holes onto the floor below, but shells came in there too, killing two more, driving the others to leap down through more holes from floor to floor.

There was dust and smoke all around the reporter, and some few feet of undamaged roof behind the chimney where he crouched. In front of it a whole floor was blown away and part of one below that so the reporter had a view of the opposite apartment where some other fighters were dancing up and down on a balcony. But some shots rang out and they disappeared into the rubble.

Then the reporter realized he was between both sides. Those who knew him were dead or gone. Those who didn't had guns laid on the building. Any move he made would bring in more rounds. There was only one way out, and that was flying through the air in death like his fighter, who had said, "You see they are stupid!"

"Maybe their God is smarter than your God," he said as if he were still talking to a live man. The reporter heard some trains rumbling overhead, jet fighters coming in, dropping cluster bombs. "On what, for God's sake, on what? You're blowing up a graveyard! The bones will fly through the air and stick in your goddam engines. In the name of God, will you stop it!" He found himself shouting into a volcano of sound. "Forgive them when they're dead, when they're all dead!"

Then he realized he was shouting hysterically so he clamped his hands over his mouth and sat with his back to the chimney looking at this patch of unharmed roof.

"They're all distracted by those planes. Those planes are my savior. There's another God at work here." So he crawled on his belly back to a jagged hole, hung down through it onto the next floor where two fighters had been killed. Then down through another ceiling hole as more jets roared in overhead and everyone who had a gun seemed to be shooting up toward a common enemy.

He reached the alley and ran along it in the mud tracks left by the pickup truck. He dodged into a bulding, went through it and the same way traversed five or six blocks away from the line of battle. Then he crouched behind a wall. Just in time, because a cluster bomb hit nearby.

In the confusion he ran toward the spot where there were casualties, knowing an ambulance would soon roar up and he could mix with the helpers, then get lost in the crowd when it dispersed, or better still, hop on the top of the ambulance like someone helping and disappear at the hospital, and so back to his bureau. So he helped with the wounded, working quickly, spread some blood on his own shirt and hands where it would show well, then got on the roof of the ambulance, which was really a hearse pressed into other service. He held on to the bars meant to hold the funeral flowers and got to the hospital from whence he could disappear.

There was no one at his bureau when he arrived. So he sat at his desk and let himself calm down. "You forgive them when they're dead," he had been told. "They won't let you when they're alive," he thought. "You need a smarter God than theirs. One who has airplanes. And can get them all shooting up in the air. So I can save myself. Save what?" There was someone's blood on his arms, on his shirt. And his head was filled with the violence of the past few hours. "My God's not smart either," he said.

48. Fighting for Life

For the Twentieth Sunday in Ordinary Time

> Do you suppose I came to establish peace on earth? No indeed, I have come to bring division. For from now on, five members of a family will be divided, three against two and two against three.
>
> LUKE 12:51–52

A man was driving home from work one day. He was behind a school bus on a two-lane road, so the stops were frequent. He didn't mind at all. The sight of young and innocent children tumbling off a bus and across lawns to peanut butter and jelly sandwiches pleased him greatly.

In his job he saw the opposite. He was an executioner for the state and in recent years had done quite a few executions. The ones he put to death were terrible people who had done terrible things. He had never executed a woman, always men, though he knew of some women. And here were these kids in front of him living in a world of peanut butter and jelly.

A car raced past him and zoomed by the stopped bus, nearly picking off two girls who were crossing the road holding each other's hands.

"Son of a bitch!" the man yelled and started to zoom out himself to catch the crazy speeder, but caught himself. He would be a second danger to those kids. And high speed chases killed the innocent.

So he edged his car out to cover the middle of the road so no one could get by while the bus was stopped. The bus started again and he could tell the bus driver had been badly frightened by the near miss. She got out at every stop and made sure the road was safe on both sides. And the man did as before, he straddled the road with his car until the bus made the last stop.

Then he drove up alongside the driver and asked: "You okay?"

"No, I'm not."

"I'd string that bastard up if I ever caught him!"

"String no one up. We're too used to killing. That's why that crazy didn't care. What's a kid or two?"

The man was silent. The woman just stood there as if she didn't want him to leave. She looked up and down the road as if the danger was not over.

"You a teacher too?" he asked.

"Yes, Primary. I get them ready for the real world."

"You'll have to tell them tomorrow about that crazy driver."

"Yes, I have to make sense out of what's senseless."

"Let me pull over," the man said, "We'll talk. I'm in no hurry. And you'll be calm in a while."

"Yes."

So the executioner pulled over and they stood near a stone wall under the trees.

"What will you tell them?" he asked.

"I'll tell them that someone didn't even know they existed. Or didn't care what happened to their lives," she said.

"That's pretty tame. I'd tell them the guy's a criminal and we gotta catch him and put him in the slammer and throw away the key, so he never does it again."

"But then they'd think of each other that way. They'd think the slammer was a solution to everything. No, kids need to know why things happen or they grow up with a hangman's mentality."

"That's what I am. I mean that's my job. I'm the state executioner. I live out this way. I see you often on this bus on my way home from work."

The woman went pale and silent. Then she said, "And you're standing here being nice to me?"

"Yes. You had a close call with a couple of your kids. I know how you feel."

The woman slowly reached out her hand and placed it on his chest and said, "Are you living and you tell me this?"

The man knew he should not have told her what his job was, but he could not change that.

"Listen, teacher, some people don't learn and you have to stop them before they kill anyone else."

"Why you?"

"I can do it. Others can't. But I've said too much about something you don't understand."

The teacher looked at him with a stillness that was like an empty room. "No, I do not understand. How could I ever explain you to them?"

"Don't try. They'll come to it on their own a little later."

"What if I asked you to stop and you did? Do you think they'd understand then?"

"Yes, but they might not understand later on when they had to decide what to do with criminals. Like that crazy that nearly ran them over."

"Well, I'm asking you to stop," she said, "so I can explain to them now that no one in their right mind would want to kill."

"Someone else would do it."

"But I don't know someone else, I know you."

The man looked up and down the road at the light traffic, and he looked at the school bus and the teacher who had her arms across her chest and seemed to be hugging something. But she was looking at him with that strange stillness of the empty room.

"All right, teacher," the man said, "I'll give it up and get another job. So you can tell those kids that no one in their right mind ever kills anyone. But you do something for me, okay?"

"What?" she asked.

"You tell me why people are not in their right mind. And if you can't, then I go back to my old job."

"That will take a long time, and I'm not sure if I can."

"I have a long time," he said, "and the job is always waiting."

49. The Man Who Wanted to Meet God

For the Twenty-first Sunday in Ordinary Time

His answer was: "Struggle to get in through the narrow door; for I tell you that many will try to enter and not be able."

LUKE 13:24

There was a man who wanted to meet God. Just out of curiosity. To see if God was really an infinite sea of love in which one could swim the crawl and backstroke and breaststroke and sidestroke. So he got a book: *Ways to Meet God*. The first way was: "Go out into a desert, real or imagined, and after all the self-love is purified, you will meet God." There was no real desert around, so he imagined one. He wiped out all the greenery, all the houses, and saw instead stretches of gravel and sand with rocky mesas rising up, and cactus plants with long needles. He even put in kangaroo rats and iguanas sunning themselves. And he sat down on a warm, imagined rock and waited for his self-love to die so he could meet God.

But he began to be happier and happier with the desert: the sky had glorious colors, the rocks were subtle shades of purple and gray, and the cactus flowers were strange and lovely, beautiful, like royal thistles. He watched the scavenger birds wheel around the vivid blue sky, passing in front of the blinding sun. "This won't do," the man said, "I love this place. It can't be real, so I can't meet God."

He left the desert and looked up the second way in the book. It said: "Give yourself totally to the service of others, and after your self-love goes you will meet God." So he went to work as an orderly in a county hospital. Because he had no training, he was put to washing the derelict men who were taken off the streets in the night by the police. He wore a special gown so the fleas would not leap on him, and on the filthy bodies brought in he used a solution that would take paint off a battleship. When he got through the layers of grime and self-soiling down to the skin, the flesh and blood, the contradiction between body and abuse of body struck him like a blow. By the time he finished cleaning them they were awake and cursing him and reaching for a pot to throw. He heard curses he never knew existed. So he strapped each clean and cursing body back on the gurney and shipped them off for a sedated sleep.

But instead of losing his self-love, he seemed to gain more. He loved the whole idea of body and he wished he could keep all the bodies in the world clean and fresh. "This is no way to meet God," he said, "not according to the book. I have to think. I'll get some lunch." So he went to the cafeteria, got himself a nice, piping hot lunch, and looked for a place to sit and think. There was only one seat free for his lunch and his book, at a table where a woman was sitting reading a newspaper over coffee. She had a stethoscope around her neck. "Must be a high-level nurse or a low-level intern," the man said to himself.

"Can I sit here?" he asked.

"Sure thing," the woman said. She moved her coffee cup closer and put the newspaper on her lap, giving him more room. "You meet God yet?" she asked.

The man nearly dropped his book and tray. "How'd you know I was looking?"

"The spaghetti doesn't hide the book," she said, "And it's quite a title, don't you think?"

The man sat down with a big smile on his face and said, "Yes, it's quite a title, but I *haven't* met God, though I've tried the first two ways, the way of the desert and the way of charity. The funny thing is, the more I fail, the happier I get. Yet I'm still curious. Is God a great sea of love you can swim in?"

"I love to swim," the woman said, "but only in saltwater and over my head. Must be a memory of the womb."

"Are you a high-level nurse or a low-level intern?" the man asked.

"Low-level intern," she said, "so I meet God every day, many times."

"How?"

"All the chief doctors are gods, and it is well to obey them."

"That does screw up the real search," he said.

"Maybe it's the other way around," she said, "Maybe God's got a book on his lunch tray called: *How to Meet the Human Species.* Very scientific book."

"You make me seem silly."

"Sorry, I meant we are the ones who get sought out, who get touched."

"My, that's interesting," he said.

"It's scary. I'm doing deliveries right now, and I swear I'm on a high after each one, problems or no problems. There's something more than a birth going on."

"You're right. I've seen a couple of births myself. And though I've been washing drunks all morning, when I get to the skin I sense they are ruining something sacred."

The woman sipped her coffee and said, "It's cold."

The man looked at his spaghetti and said, "It's cold, too." They both laughed, and she said, "Talk about God, and things get cold."

"Well, that's the next suggestion in the book," he said, "It says, 'Talk to people about God.' That doesn't work either."

"Well, maybe it does. I've enjoyed this conversation enormously."

"But I've only enjoyed you. It was the same thing with suggestion one: I loved the desert. And with suggestion two: I loved the derelicts. And now this."

"Well, I guess if you love deserts and derelicts and dames you are not far from the kingdom. We'll just have to do, until the real thing comes along. What about lunch tomorrow?"

"Yes, lunch," he answered, "And funny thing. The next suggestion in the book is: 'Live for tomorrow and you will meet God.'"

"Sounds like a Chinese fortune cookie," she said.

50. When the Priest's Away . . .

For the Twenty-second Sunday in Ordinary Time

Remember where you stand: not before the palpable, blazing fire of Sinai, with the darkness, gloom, and whirlwind, the trumpet-blast and the oracular voice, which they heard, and begged to hear no more;
HEBREWS 12:18–19

A woman had a vision one day. It was of a bottle of perfume that had been broken and left lying on the sidewalk. The air around it was filled with a delicate scent. But the broken pieces were sharp and dangerous to anyone who touched them. "What does this mean?" the woman asked herself. She did not know. "I'd better go ask a priest." So she went to the priest house and rang the doorbell.

The housekeeper answered, and the woman said, "I'd like to see a priest."

"Any particular one?" the housekeeper asked.

"Someone good with visions."

"None of them are good with visions," the housekeeper said, "unless it's visions of impending doom, like the boiler blowing up or the roof leaking. Anyway, what kind of vision is it?"

"Well, it's about a broken bottle of perfume on a sidewalk, all sharp-edged fragments, but a beautiful scent in the air all around."

"Oh dear," said the housekeeper, "that sounds like a broken woman! Oh, the pity! Are you a broken woman?"

"No," the woman answered, "not at all. I'm successful and I'm happy."

"Then it must be that you're going to be broken. It'll do a lot of good for others, but none for yourself."

"What makes you say that? It's almost too simple!"

"Well, maybe I am talking about myself," the housekeeper said, "This is one of those days when I feel like broken dishes, never mind a bottle of perfume. Come in and I'll see if I can scare up a priest."

"You think one of them will help?" the woman asked.

"I don't know. You're the first one ever to come with a vision. It's mainly funerals and weddings around here. What kind of perfume was it?"

"I don't know. It was a light scent, like dried flowers. It wasn't intrusive; I scarcely noticed it as it surrounded me."

"It's a lot like yourself," the housekeeper said, "But the sharp edges on the broken bottle are not. Maybe it means Jesus. This is Lent, you know, when he is broken on the cross and helps everybody. Or maybe it means the church. The old thing has to be busted if its ever going to spread and do good! Well, the pastor's not in. I think he's out with the sexton buying tulip bulbs for the spring. Do you want some tea?"

"No, thanks. Maybe I shouldn't bother anybody. It's just that everything around me is filled with the scent of dried flowers and yet everything seems to have sharp edges, as if just broken open and left lying. And it's all so dangerous and beautiful at the same time. I don't know what to do."

"Sit. I'll ring the curate. I call him curate still. It's a great name. This one knows more than God, so if he's in you'll find out what the vision means. What color was the bottle?"

"It was ivory, like porcelain, like something the Magi would carry to Bethlehem. And it glowed in the light. Just as everything glows in the light right now."

"You don't think it's a vision of God, do you?" the housekeeper asked.

"Why would it be?"

"The everything," the housekeeper said, "the everything broken open and giving off a beautiful scent and yet too dangerous to touch. Must be God!"

"Who taught you things like that?"

"You learn things on your own. There's no curate in the house. He must be over after his car in the garage. His fan belt is screeching. Where will I look now? I don't want you leaving here. All you have is my blab and no solution."

"I'll come back when a priest is in," the woman said, "But I don't know what to do till then. The scent is so strong, and the edges so sharp."

"I can see it too. They'll lock us both up."

"I didn't mean to harm you," the woman said.

"You didn't harm me. I haven't felt so alive since I started working here. If we can just get one of them to say it means Jesus or God we're onto a great vision."

"And what if we can't?"

"Then we're stuck with the broken woman. That may be the best we can do."

"Shall I come back?" the woman said.

"Yes," the housekeeper said, "at least for tea."

51. A Trolley-Car Priest

For the Twenty-third Sunday in Ordinary Time

> With difficulty we guess even at things on earth, and laboriously find out what lies before our feet; and who has ever traced out what is in heaven?
> WISDOM 9:16

A woman was waiting for the trolley in the subway one evening. The trolley did not come. So she said to herself, "I'll be like Job, very patient, so when the trolley comes, I won't be a wreck with rage." Ten minutes went by and the trolley did not come. And she was nearly a wreck with rage. So she said, "I need the patience of Jesus on the Cross." For the next ten minutes, the patience of Jesus on the Cross worked. But the trolley did not come. So she said, "I need the wisdom of God or I'll pitch that trolley into the sea." For the next ten minutes the wisdom of God worked. But the trolley did not come. In the next ten minutes she became a wreck with rage. And then the trolley came. So she said to the driver, "Why were you so late?"

He said, "I'm not late, I'm right on time!"

She said, "I waited forty minutes!"

He said, "*I* haven't."

The woman knew what a stone wall was, so she backed away. She tripped over somebody's cowboy boots stuck out in the aisle and then lurched into someone carrying a baby and said, "Sorry! sorry!" Then she dropped her handbag into a shuffle of feet and couldn't pick it up because the trolley was jouncing left to right on a stretch of bad track. She retrieved the handbag, then gripped the handle on the back of a seat and thought, "This is too small a ride for so much rage!"

She thought of the old vaudeville joke: "Would you hit a woman with a baby? No, I'd hit her with a brick." And her rage broke down. She had just hit a woman with a baby. With herself. Then she saw the headlines of a newspaper the man in the seat was reading: *Parents Picket AIDS Pupil!* And: *Reagan Reads Russians Riot Act!* Too many words. And: *Bomb Blasts Beirut Bistro!* Oh, God! Are there any bistros left?" she wondered. And: *Pope Bars Women Priests. Pushes for Peace!*

"He's a trolley driver," she thought, "I'd push for peace, but I wouldn't do it by barring women priests. In fact I might use women priests to push for peace. That's it! I'd use women priests to cool off those parents panicked over AIDS. And I'd use women priests to take the riot out of the Russians.

"And I'd use women priests to drive this damn trolley. What's he stopping for now? The tunnel is clear to kingdom come." Then she began to feel elation come over her. She was turning into a woman priest on a stalled trolley in an empty subway. She thought, "I can absorb the driver's lie. I can put it with my own lies. Then he'd really know I knew. I can tell that woman what a beautiful baby she has. I can take those parents' fears and put them in with my own and find that maybe there's something more important than life. And I can tell the military they have weapons enough to blow God out of the sky. And I can tell Beirut what's happened. You've blown three gods out of the sky. And I can tell the pope that he came from a woman, that he prays to one now, and maybe God's the woman he'll have to live with after he dies!

"A trolley car priest, that's what I am! I have to forgive a lie with my own lies. I have to calm fears with my own fears. And push for peace by hitting people with a baby not a brick. But I'm like a bullet in the barrel of a gun in this subway, so mad I could kill somebody. And if I ever do I'm dead myself. So I want wars to stop."

The trolley started wth a lurch, and she stepped back on someone's foot. He looked like a football tackle, so tall his head touched the ceiling. She had to look up to say, "I'm sorry."

"That's OK," he said, "You look a little shaken. You can hold on to me if you want. I'm good at holding too."

"No," she said, "thanks though. I'd better learn to stand for myself."

52. The Mannequin's Bus

For the Twenty-fourth Sunday in Ordinary Time

And when she has, she calls her friends and neighbours together, and says, "Rejoice with me! I have found the piece that I lost." In the same way, I tell you, there is joy among the angels of God over one sinner who repents.

LUKE 15:9–10

There was a young woman who became bald. In a short time. No one could explain why. Until they did, she was faced with desperate measures at desperate costs to try and restore what had been a beautiful head of hair. She tried wigs. She tried living as a recluse. One day as she stood before her mirror to put on her wig she noticed that her head was beautifully shaped. She looked like a mannequin but alive. She had no lines to her face, no freckles, just smooth skin wrapped around a perfect skull. She still had eyebrows and long lashes. "I'll just live this way," she thought. "Outdoors, indoors, no wig, no hat. Maybe use dark eye makeup. And just a touch of lipstick. No earrings."

So she went to work that way. And people stared in fascination. "They think I'm a belly dancer," she thought, "or a model for necklaces, diamonds, pearls. Maybe I'm punk. No, too neat for punk. Maybe a hooker. That's it. They're wondering how much. Can they afford it? I'm on the street—Can't be too much. Oh, no! I'm Squeaky from the Manson gang. Or maybe they think I sold my hair for a wig to pick up some extra change. They just stare and stare." She got to her bus stop as the bus came. She lived in a government town and people from all walks of life rode the bus. She saw the driver every day.

He took one look and said, "Geez, what'd you do?"

"Decided to face it," she said as she showed him her pass and sat where he could hear.

"Oh mother, face what?" he said and swung the bus back into traffic.

"That I'm bald. Nothing I can do. So I'll live with it. No more disguises," she said.

"Boy, you look so good I can hardly drive this thing."

"You scare me to death," said a woman across the aisle. "I'd jump off a bridge. Or my man would throw me off."

"You'll catch a cold," said a little kid with a big grin, "catch a cold."

"I'll catch you," said the bald-headed woman.

The kid climbed up his mother's leg.

"They'll think something else," the mother said.

"Took me five seconds to find out," the bald woman said.

"Let me just touch you," an old man said, "I never, I never . . ." and he reached a shaky hand from where he stood in the aisle.

"Sit," said the driver, "or you'll never touch nothin' again."

"Ain't no seat," said the old man. "Here," said the bald woman.

"No, here," said the mother, "the boy can stand."

"I never, I never . . ." said the old man with an enormous smile. He sat and just stroked the woman's hand. "Fine," he said, "fine!"

The driver hit the brakes and yelled, "Sunofabitch Mercedes!"

A man ended up in the bald woman's lap, briefcase and newspaper still clutched tight. "I'm sorry," he said, "I should look what I'm doing."

"He was staring," said the kid with the grin.

Back on his feet, the man looked sheepish.

"Yes," he said. "It's perfect. 'I never' either. I've taken this bus ten years."

The driver hit the horn. "Goddam Rolls! British think they can drive both sides."

"You'll get ulcers," the bald woman said.

"He's still staring," said the kid with the grin.

"Shush," said his mother. "Someone will step on you. Gone like a bug."

"I am staring," said the man, "You are truly beautiful. This is no come-on. I work in the National Gallery. I'm in charge of portraits."

"You're not going to put me on a wall?"

"No," he said, "I wish you were my protocol officer. To show bigwigs around." He blushed at the pun.

The driver hit the horn and the brakes at the same time. "Stupid Caddy, go make a law and shove it!"

"I have a job," the woman said, "I'm a systems analyst for the GAO."

The old man laughed and stroked her hand. "I never, I never . . ." Then he said to the driver, "Gotta get out, gotta get out . . ."

"It's too soon," said the driver, "She catches you drinkin', she'll whack you one."

"I got mints all over me," the old man said.

"I work with numbers, not faces, it's good money," the bald woman said.

"They'll have their numbers all screwed up today," the driver said. "Want me to let you off here? There's a Caddy and a Rolls in a beautiful smashup ahead. Nobody moves for a while. Okay, everybody, this is it for an hour! Anybody who wants to can walk!"

"See you," said the bald woman as she got off.

"See you first," said the driver.

She walked along beside the stuck cars, their chauffeurs out and their passengers on the phones inside. Some horns beeped. Some windows slid down.

"Wait up," mumbled a voice behind her. It was the portrait man. His paper was in his mouth, one hand held the briefcase, the other buttoned his trenchcoat. "I need someone for the truth. And it's art. And it's people open the way they never are."

"And I need someone who can smell a crook in a column of figures. Who can spot a lie in a printout," the bald woman said, "like someone who can smell water with their skin."

"But this is in charge of beauty," he said, "not the beasts."

"I'll bet many a beast walks in there."

"Yes, I guess, but you have a way with beasts, like Orpheus."

"How would you know?"

"That whole bus," he said.

"And what about my brain?"

"Orpheus *was* a brain," he said, "Everybody else was dumb."

53. An Eye Examination

For the Twenty-fifth Sunday in Ordinary Time

> When he comes, he will confute the world, and show where wrong and right and judgment lie.
>
> JOHN 16:8

There was a woman who wanted to make a dent in life. "I can't go the centerfold route," she thought, "someone will discover it when I'm president. Besides, who wants to dent somebody's eyes? One blink and the dent is gone. I'll use my mind. Let's see, nuclear physics, that's either bombs or meltdowns. I'd worry either way." She worked her way like that through medicine, law, art, and fashion designing. She even thought of being a priest in some church, but then she thought, "People blink in churches too, and you're gone. That leaves marriage, a nunnery, or what else? A truth no one else knows. That's it! Now what does no one else know? Who I am! That's it! And what a dent I'll make when people find out. I'll start small. I have two different colored eyes. I'll see if people notice. Make it a three-second contest for ten dollars."

So she stepped up to a man and said, "I'll give you ten dollars if in three seconds you can tell me what is distinctive about me."

The man looked quickly and said, "You've got two different-colored eyes, one brown, one blue."

"My, you did it," she said. "Here's your money. I thought no one would notice."

"I'll give it back to you," he said, "if in three seconds you can say what's distinctive about me."

"There's nothing distinctive about you," the woman said after a quick look.

"Right," the man said, "Here's your money back. I'm a secret service man and I'm supposed to blend in anywhere, not be noticed."

"Secret service for what?" the woman asked.

"To keep people from getting shot."

"How do you do that?"

"You either shoot first or *get* shot," the man said.

"You do this every day?"

"Nearly."

"Is that why you noticed my eyes right away?" she asked.

"Yes," he said, "I watch eyes all the time. They're the windows of the soul. How's that for a new thought!"

"Then tell me what you see in mine."

"For how much?"

"For ten dollars."

"Okay," he said, "I see someone who wants to make a dent in the world and wants to use her mind to do so."

"Am I that transparent?" she asked.

"To me you are. Who else thinks up a game like that and tests it on the first person she meets?"

"I could have been a prostitute."

"No."

"I could have been a broadcaster and had a TV crew hidden in those bushes."

"No."

"I could have been a college girl being hazed for a sorority."

"No, your body is quiet, your questions are unprepared, and you're too old for hazing. You want to make a dent in the world, and you want to use your head."

"How do I do that?" she asked, "My first attempt has failed."

He said, "You have to know what's distinctive about other people, not what's distinctive about yourself."

"I could never have guessed you were a secret service man and you either killed or got killed. And I could never have guessed you could read the color of people's eyes."

"That's not true," he said.

"How is it not true?" she asked.

"Look at my eyes."

"Yes. Oh. One is gray and one is green. I should have seen."

"Now look behind me at who is talking in the doorway of that shop."

"Oh. That's the president, and that's the president's wife. And somebody I don't know." Then she froze. "Surely you don't think . . ." she began.

"I surely don't," he said, "And I'll move out of the way to prove it."

"I guess my questioning you was pretty dangerous."

"No, it was my answering you that was dangerous."

"That's what you suggest I do, answer," she said.

"Yes."

"Will that make a dent in life?"

"Yes, but different than mine."

"How so?" she asked.

"Nothing to do with bullets," he said.

54. Dives the Rich Man and How He Ended

For the Twenty-sixth Sunday in Ordinary Time

But that is not all: there is a great chasm fixed between us; no one from our side who wants to reach you can cross it, and none may pass from your side to us.

LUKE 16:26

A rich man went to church one day. He was middle aged and a bachelor. He figured he should get some of his childhood back. Make life a little less cold and calculating. The scripture read was about Dives the rich man and Lazarus the poor, with the same ending sure enough, Dives poor and in hell and Lazarus rich and in heaven. "But wait a minute," the modern rich man thought to himself, "Abraham was just as stingy about heaven as Dives was about earth. The only thing anyone wants to share is hell." Then the man laughed to himself, "I could sure raise hell with money."

When the collection plate came he floated a thousand-dollar bill on top of the envelopes and petty cash. He saw the usher twitch with surprise. "Bet that bill doesn't make it home," the man thought. Then he was ashamed at his own arrogance. "I can't raise hell if I have no money," he said to himself. He left church and within a few day's time gave away all his money, to people who should get it and people who shouldn't. "Okay, Lazarus," he said to himself, "now what?"

He saw a sign across the street that said, "Short-Order Cook Wanted." He loved to cook, so he went over to the old-fashioned diner and got the job, though the owner was uneasy about his soft, white hands. Within a week he had figured out a new kind of hamburger, the meat rolled like a fat hot dog around an unexpected tube of cheese that could be filled with mustard or relish or onions or catsup. The bun was a roll the fitted the burger perfectly. The whole thing was bite-size, except for kids. You never ran out of meat before you ran out of bread. And you peeled the napkin back like a banana so you never got dripped on.

The owner was wild with excitement. Business boomed. He opened another diner, then another, and another, then sold out for a fortune to a big-name company and gave the inventor a third of the profit. So the rich man/poor man was rich again. He could hear Dives laughing at him and saying, "I'm keeping a seat free."

Then the rich man gave his third away again, to those who should get it and to those who shouldn't. "This time I go begging," he said. "Nothing but quarters that way." So he begged with his dirty cap in one hand and a pleading half-smile on his face.

One day someone dropped a lottery ticket in his cap and said, "Good luck, buddy, nothing for me, might be something for you." Sure enough, in ten days the ticket was worth ten million dollars.

The man turned it in and was rich again. And he heard Dives down in hell laughing even harder: "I'll save you two seats! They feed you that money every year for twenty years. You can't give it away! Har, har, har!"

"Say," said the man to Dives, "I thought you wanted people out of hell?"

"Misery loves company," said Dives.

"I could send you a lot of company. I tell you what, give me one good idea on how to use this money, and I'll get you out myself."

"I haven't thought about money in years. I'm up to my ass in flames. What about burn victims?"

"I've done that," the rich man said, "What else are you up to your ass in?"

"There's smoke," Dives said, "and the place is polluted, and there's war, and hatred by the ton, and everybody's starved."

"I've done that."

"Well, there's one thing left, but I can't tell you. I explode if I try, and it takes me weeks to find all the pieces."

"Ah," said the rich man, "you mean make money love."

"Stop, you'll blow my eardrums."

"Make money love, how do I do that?"

"Nobody's supposed to know. You remember that thousand you laid on the plate? That's an extra log on the fire."

"It figures," the rich man said. "What about the hamburger money?"

"That's just a few toothpicks."

"So if I do some good with this stuff and nobody knows, then that's love?"

"Ouch! You've cracked my skull like a melon."

"That means I'm loving something other than my own soul?"

"Ow! There goes an arm and a leg!"

"And that means I have to know what I love and who?"

"Jeekers," said Dives, "my ass is shot off. Will you stop using that word! You're supposed to get me out of here in one piece!"

"People have to know it's love or all hell breaks loose."

"I'm gone," Dives said, "all I am is a voice, but I'm going to haunt you for this, you bastard, wherever you go."

"You'd love to do that wouldn't you?"

"Love to, love to," said Dives. Then his voice was gone.

The rich man changed his name. Nobody knew where he had come from. And nobody knew where he went.

55. A Superior Being

For the Twenty-seventh Sunday in Ordinary Time

Guard the treasure put into our charge, with the help of the Holy Spirit dwelling within us.

2 TIMOTHY 1:14

A man was going through customs late one evening in a foreign city. He had two bags plus a backpack with stuff for his students. He was a teacher on his way to teach at a university. No one stopped him as he walked slowly through the customs corridor.

He had just seen a black man put through the wringer at passport control. Now he saw an Indian family asked to open all their luggage and to show their return flight tickets. Yet he with his white face and western dress walked through unchallenged, out onto the nearly empty concourse.

"I'm a superior being," he thought, "I could be carrying a homemade atom bomb. Everything around serves me. For money, yes. But I'm what money is for." He looked for a money exchange, got the foreign currency, then bought a bus ticket for downtown Rome. As he sat waiting to start, a woman with a puzzled look got on the wrong end of the bus, came to him and asked in English but with a foreign accent, "Does this bus go into Rome?"

"Yes," he said. And she left him wondering why she had spoken in English. The bus trip was a series of mad swings around traffic circles, quick lurches to avoid hitting cars, squealing of brakes at stop lights, chugging starts to beat others into one lane. "Superior being," he thought, "superior dice. Superior profit. I'll beat this system." So in town, as he got off the bus, he refused the taxi drivers who could not believe his refusal and he dragged his superior being to a local bus. It was loaded with young Scandinavians who took up nearly all the seats. An Indian woman holding a baby got on, her mother with her, and immediately the teacher leading the group said, "Olaf," and a young man got up from his seat and gave it graciously to the Indian woman. Another got up and gave the grandmother a seat.

"And I'm afraid to give a bum a nickel," the man said to himself. "A superior being is someone with a tight fist. I've got to let myself be stopped from now on. But there are some fake stories: 'I have a fixed-date airplane ticket and someone stole my money.' 'I have to eat for three days before my plane leaves.' Or 'I'm here to study architecture, and someone lifted my wallet at the railroad station.'"

But then the man remembered what he had been told: Don't stop for people who beg. Especially for gypsies. Most especially for gypsy children. You'll be cleaned out in two seconds, including the watch on your wrist. So the man felt very exposed as the bus bounced and jolted toward the center of town. "I do have to go through customs all the time," he thought. "People examine you for everything."

He saw a young woman looking at him from the front of the bus. She was handsome, blond, blue-eyed. She had her arm around a young man who was seated on the floor. Yet she looked at him, and looked. He loved it, but knew no reason why a young woman with a young man should look at an older man with a stack of bags. "And I'll never know," he thought, as she looked away. "Few people look at me anymore just for fun. When I was handsome they looked all the time."

The bus took a hard turn left and headed down the hill to the piazza where Mussolini used to address mass audiences from a balcony.

"My stop," the man realized. "I'll have to go out the wrong door. I'll never make it through this crowd with three bags." So when the bus stopped, he left through the back and got to the sidewalk, where he put himself in some order before walking to his lodgings.

"When I get touched by a love, I give away the world," he thought. "I guess that's flattery. Flattery is its own reward. But I would like to be touched by a love all the time. I'm touched by lies most often, sometimes by a little lust." He thought of his balding head. He felt for the bulge of his wallet and passport, shifted his return ticked to an outside pocket so it wouldn't get soaked with sweat. "And I'm touched by misery and violence." He put down his bags for a minute to get circulation back in his hands. "And I'm touched by egotists who want me to look adoringly at the idols they have become."

Ahead of him was the doorway of the university where he was to teach. "But if it were just love, I'd do things I never thought of doing." He stopped for another minute. "You never treat superior beings with love," he thought. He picked up his bags again. They were too heavy and he knew it. "It's for love," he thought, "but who's going to know?"

56. Great Danes and Shitty Shoes

For the Twenty-eighth Sunday in Ordinary Time

If we are faithless, he keeps faith,
for he cannot deny himself.

2 TIMOTHY 2:13

A man stepped on a dog turd one bad day in his life. That broke the spell of the bad day for him. He had to clown-walk away, like Chaplin, on one heel. "It must have been a Great Dane," he said to himself, "Some notorious criminal's. One the police wouldn't dare arrest." So the man looked for a puddle, saw one in the gutter just outside his apartment, stuck his foot in it and walked forward and backward like someone with a short leg as he tried to get rid of the dog dirt.

Then he was ashamed of mocking a human defect, so he stopped, saw some grass, went over to it, and began to scrape the shoe. "I'm like a good dog now," he said to himself, "burying its own poop."

"You should wear high heels," he heard a woman say, "you land on less."

"You know this experience?" he asked.

The woman had a toy poodle on a leash. Its bark was like a hard sneeze. "I always clean it up," the woman said, "But a woman's shoes do pick up less."

"Then I'd like to be in a woman's shoes." He had just changed a yard of grass from green to brown.

"It's like walking a tightrope," she said.

"I just fell off one," he said, "Broke a couple of dreams."

"Well, those are women's shoes," she said, "a couple of dreams."

"You're a nun. You've got a cross."

"Right. You're not so blind."

"You're a nun with a dog, a toy poodle?"

"Right. The dog likes me. It's my sister's, and she's in Mexico on the beach with her whole family. The dog's mine for a month. Her apartment too."

"You should have more than a dog," he said, "You should have wisdom and tell me why women want divorces and why priests who tell them no kick each other out of churches. I think the women should kick the men out of the churches, and the priests should get divorces. Then everybody would be free of everybody else."

"But not poodles," the nun said.

"Right." The man lifted his foot like a blacksmith looking at a hoof. "Clean," he said, "clean at last."

"What's the woman want to divorce you for?" the nun asked.

"She says I'm a stranger."

"Well, that's one way to get you home. Unless she's got somebody else?"

"No, no one else, just me, she's too unhappy. She's right, I've been making a fortune, like a fanatic. You saw me scrape this shoe. Fanatic!"

"You have to unfanaticize. I don't mean leave the shit on your shoe. That makes fanatics of everybody else. They want you to be alone."

"Alone is bad," he said.

"Yes. You lose who you are."

"That's funny from you. You're supposed to be alone. I'm surprised at the dog."

"Wrong," she said, "alone is dead. That's why the priests are kicking each other out. What's dead doesn't disagree."

"I'm glad I didn't marry a woman priest. I'd have been out a long time ago."

"We need new priests," the nun said. "We need women, women who love to disagree."

"Not you. You're easygoing."

"No, not me. I see things I wouldn't want to miss, things people hide from priests."

"I should get my wife to talk to you."

"You might lose her faster."

"Right," the man said, "Don't talk to her. Talk to me. How do I get unfanaticized so she doesn't want me to be alone for good?" He looked at his shoe to be sure it was clean.

"Stop talking to me," the nun said.

"Right. And start talking to her. And what about? Anything, right? Great Danes and shitty shoes. And you, you'll be alone again?"

"No," the nun said, "Something always happens when I walk this dog. Last time it was a woman who never saw her man. Time before it was a priest out walking *his* dog. A Great Dane."

57. The Big Lie

For the Twenty-ninth Sunday in Ordinary Time

Proclaim the message, press it home on all occasions, convenient or inconvenient, use argument, reproof, and appeal, with all the patience that the work of teaching requires.

2 TIMOTHY 4:2

There was a man who had a crazy job. He had to take intelligence information on several world situations and draw up the worst possible interpretation of that information. Then he had to hand it on to a crucial advisor. Someone else in the office had to draw up the best possible interpretation and hand that on. So the man felt free to imagine the worst.

It was not lying, it was make-believe of a very high order, and the man loved doing it. There could be nuclear bombs beneath those piles of grain, or in the jungles there could be gun-running or dope-smuggling serious enough to change the world order. Or the weight of population could become so great that hordes of people would cross continents like locusts, devouring every-thing before them or leaving every ditch filled with death and disease.

Some days he longed to read the best-case scenarios, but he was not allowed that lest it spoil the sharpness of the worst-case vision. But one day he began to notice that certain of his phrases were being used in news releases. They were neat phrases, he thought, and he began to feel a little pride. He loved language the way a lion tamer loves the beasts that he has trained to jump through flaming hoops.

Later the man began to see whole scenarios released to the press, stories about small events to be sure, but almost word for word what he had concocted and sent up to the advisor. He became uneasy. Now his private fictions were becoming public facts. And he noticed that the woman who did the best-case scenarios had been transferred out and was now working for Defense.

More and more requests came to his desk asking for his scenarios. He thought, "I'll be the cause of disaster! Someone has forgotten what I'm doing and is taking it for the straight-out truth." This was a worst-case scenario he had never dreamed of. The man was not a liar. "I'd better stop," he thought. Then: "They will just get someone else. Someone wants to do horrible damage somewhere, it almost doesn't seem to matter where. Someone like a sleepwalker. I'd better stop that someone." So he thought for a long time. "I'm too small to spill the beans, I'll have to build my scenarios slowly so the one who uses them will look more and more crazy, then people will surely know and this whole business will stop."

He began to slip in words and phrases right out of *Mein Kampf* and waited for people to spot them and call a halt to the one who issued the press releases. But nothing happened. The man became more frightened. So he added words from Mao Tse Tung's little red book, splicing them in with the *Mein Kampf* words. Still no one seemed to notice really, though some shrill voices began to rise from the left, but they were called crazy.

"I'm going in the wrong direction," the man thought. "I have to make someone sound like Mother Theresa holding a dying baby. And yet act like Genghis Khan at his worst." So he began to suggest in his scenarios that peace was the worst thing that could happen in several countries, that talk of peace would provoke internal upheavals. He began to slide into his reports words from TV evangelists and from papal documents. The press releases slowed down, but some of his old scenarios lingered in the air. So more and more he showed that peace would be the worst possible scenario and talk of peace would unleash reactionary forces.

Slowly the press releases changed, and he heard his new worst-case scenarios showing up under words suggesting peace. Then it struck him with horror that no one thought the new voice was crazy. Except some voices on the right. They were shrill too, considered mad. But the voice that issued the press releases was considered as sane as ever.

"No one knows what a lie is anymore," he thought. "No one knows who's crazy. Except me. And I'm hired to be a crazy liar. Except I'm not anymore. The only way out of this is to turn myself in as a spy and take that advisor out with me. But I don't know enough to carry it off." Then something came to him. His name was really not known up above, just his material. If he could switch positions with the woman who had done the best-case scenarios, then the material that went up would surely make the advisor seem to be crazy, or to be a prophet. Either way the situation was saved.

But he was wrong. He was not unknown. He was appointed to be the advisor, a solution he had never thought of. The other advisor had been made chief. "I know nothing but my own fictions," he thought, "I have to choose the right one. Sound like Genghis Khan and act like Mother Theresa. I'll fool everybody that way. But I'd better get someone at this desk who knows what a fiction is. Or I'll end up fooled too."

So he called Defense, but the woman he wanted had been shifted to Education. At Education they told him she had been shifted to Immigration. He called there, but she had been shifted to Budget. He finally got her at Commerce, and his panic subsided. But she would not take the job until he explained to her all that had happened. There was a long pause on the phone. Then she said, "I can do the same to you!"

"Yes, after a while you can," he said.

"What's the worst that can happen to me if I do? Will I forget I'm a crazy liar?"

"No," he said, "the worst is if I forget."

58. A Woman's Touch

For the Thirtieth Sunday in Ordinary Time

> When men cry for help, the LORD
>   hears them
> and sets them free from all their
>   troubles.
> The LORD is close to those whose
>   courage is broken
> and he saves those whose spirit is
>   crushed.
>
> PSALM 34:17-18

A woman was returning from a famine in Africa. She was a nurse and specialized in the newborn. The famine was nearly over and the newborn mostly dead, but some had survived, so there would be a new generation in a few years to populate the edge of that desert. "In twenty years' time, I won't be able to do this again," she thought. She saw Kilimanjaro out the window, the main peak. She knew that mountain. She had read a book by a climber who broke his leg at the ankle up on the soft glacier of that mountain and had been all but abandoned by his fellow climber, who supposedly had gone for help. It was a story of survival she would never forget.

She remembered the Hemingway piece about the skeleton of the leopard found far above the tree line, where leopards never go. "A mystical leopard looking to eat God," she thought. She could see the steaming jungle at Kilimanjaro's base and its frozen top out of reach of any green life. "All I think about is the power to survive," she said half aloud.

"Now you do," said the woman beside her, an old woman with a voice almost as deep as a man's. "But that changes later when everyone you know is gone."

The nurse was startled a bit, then laughed and looked at the woman, who was leaning to see the mountain also. Her face was filled with lines, but there was a female power to it that was unmistakable.

The old woman said, "You're on top, you can see the whole world, you're alone, and there's nothing you can do with what you know."

"Someone can always live because of you," the nurse said.

They both fell silent, what the nurse had said was so powerful. The mountain was up ahead of them. And the old woman's face was nearly touching the younger woman's. And the mountain's shadow to the west was still purple from the morning light. The nurse put her hand up and moved the old woman's face until it met her own. She held it there until the mountain was alongside of them. Then she let her hand drop.

"I never knew there was anything ahead of me," the old woman said. "I came back here for a last look. I was an old colonial. I had everything. Even after I left I had everything. But when the people go, there's nothing. Now that's not true. You have life in your hands."

"It's been left there," the nurse said.

"Tell me what that means."

"It means I saw a lot of babies out in the famine to the east of here. They left their lives with me as they died. This whole world is dripping with life. But only for some. Not for others. Like the jungle at the base of that brute of a mountain."

"You are going home now?" the old woman asked.

"Yes. I'm a specialist. And back home we save most of the babies. Some just fit in the palm of your hand when you get them."

"You seem to be able to touch anything. I've got these old claws from Macbeth."

The nurse laughed and said, "Do we all turn into witches and hags and crones?"

"No," the old woman said, "but I do wish I had warm hands. I wish I could touch the way you do. Especially new life."

The nurse looked at her own hands, and they began to shake because of what she had just been through. "Why don't you hold me," she said to the old woman. "There's death in my hands too."

So the old woman reached across and took the nurse's two hands in her own.

And the nurse said, "I can get on this plane and go home. There are a million women back there who cannot leave. I am so happy I am not one of them. I don't know what I would do if I were dry and someone was still trying to suck some life from me. I am happy I know what I know up here at 35,000 feet and going 500 miles an hour. If we just get beyond the first few years we have a chance to live. We can take almost anything."

"Maybe," the old woman said. "Anyway, I'll now find out. My parents both lost their powers before they died. I promised myself if that happened to me, I'd walk into the sea. Like Alfonsina Storni. You know of her?"

"I think so. Her lover betrayed her and she couldn't live."

"Yes. It's as if life betrays you at the end. Only you can't walk anywhere, never mind into the sea."

"So you won't now?"

"I would betray you if I did."

The nurse's hands stopped shaking. They both sensed it.

"You have taken these deaths from me," the nurse said, "Maybe you shouldn't."

And the old woman said, "It's not your time for them yet. It is mine." She reached up, touched the nurse's face, and said, "Maybe death is not the last thing we touch."

"Maybe it is," the nurse said, "but it leaves us something."

The mountain was behind them now. They could still see its shadow though, like a long net cast on the waters of a lake. They watched it drawing in.

59. See Jerusalem and Die!

For the Dedication of St. John Lateran

> For all existing things are dear to thee and thou hatest nothing that thou hast created—why else wouldst thou have made it? How could anything have continued in existence, had it not been thy will? How could it have endured unless called into being by thee?
>
> WISDOM 11:24–25

A man was standing in the Temple in Jerusalem one day. He was looking north to the Mosque of Omar. It was framed in the archways where the scales for the Last Judgment would hang to weigh all the souls against the truth. To his left outside the Temple was the Wailing Wall. He could hear chanting. Beyond the wall to the West was the tower of the Lutheran Church, near the site of Calvary and the empty tomb. The man's arms were crossed in front of him. He was motionless before the beauty of the scene, the gold Dome of the Rock with its crescent moon on top, the many-sided building below with its exquisite Arabic script from the Koran, the beautiful blue and white tile-work of the walls.

The sky was deep and clear and the air was fresh. An Arab guard came up to him slowly and sternly and said in awkward English, "What are you doing?"

"I'm looking at the beauty of the Mosque," the man answered.

"Is that all?" The guard's hand was resting on the heel of a .45 Colt automatic.

"Yes." The man almost said, "I know enough not to pray in your temple."

The guard moved slowly away. The man stood there a little longer. The beauty was gone and the savagery of Jerusalem was in its place. He felt another presence beside him. A woman was standing there, her shoulder almost touching his, looking north. She said, "He would have killed you if you had been praying."

"I know. If you pray you claim where you stand for your God."

"Something even worse. You claim it for yourself. And that's murder here."

"You're talking to me for a reason," he said.

"Yes." she said, "Just to be free of all this conflict. Maybe just to live with the beauty of things, if I can. You were looking at that beauty."

"Are you from this country?"

"Yes, I am now. I came a few years ago to be with my own people. But that's as hard as living with people not my own."

"Why do you come here?" he asked.

"So I don't have to believe. This way I can see things as they are, I can feel them as wind and rock and design and flesh. I don't have to hate. I don't have to love. I can just be."

"God will be mad at you for that," the man said.

"He's got bigger things to be mad at than me," she answered. "You a Christian?"

"Easy enough to tell, isn't it?"

"Yes. For Jews and Arabs, God gets mad at whole peoples. For Christians, at boys and girls who don't say their prayers."

"I think we have God tamed," the man said. "There is only a spanking for not saying prayers, not some—" He stopped abruptly.

"Holocaust?"

"Yes. I guess the only God I believe in is the God of night prayers: 'Take care of my mummy and my daddy and my dog who stepped on a nail.' And I don't expect him even to do that."

"You sound like you miss him."

"I miss something. Something innocent. But innocence is as dead as my dog, and my mummy, and my daddy."

"I wish God were a great roaring drunk," she said, "who made everybody laugh until they were sick and had to go out for air."

"Falstaff."

"Oh no! Just a big innocent fool who didn't know what he just drank and suddenly remembers every joke he ever heard. Not a mean drunk."

"Arabs wouldn't laugh, most Christians wouldn't either."

"Then maybe someone who just danced and sang himself silly, at a wedding, a teetotaler. But someone with a passion for joy." She gagged as she said that. "This whole city is screaming for some joy!"

"And it has none?" the man asked.

"Oh, it's flooded with it, but the city hates it."

"You lost me," he said.

"Well, did you see the posters of a young woman in a bathing suit put up in all the bus stops? Vacation posters for the Gulf of Aqaba?"

"Yes."

"Every religion in this town hates the woman on that poster and wants to rip it right off those stops, because her body is young and joyful."

"How do you know it is?" he asked.

"Well look at me," she said, "Even if I am wearing baggy clothes."

"I guess I didn't notice your face on the poster," he said, "I'm among the enemy."

"You notice it now?"

"Yes."

"You like it?"

"Yes."

"It fits the body?" she asked.

"Yes."

"There's a whole world of women here," she said. "Some of us look like clouds and some of us look like camels, but there's a joy in us, believe me, only it's wrapped as tight as Pharoah in his tomb."

"This place would have to give up all belief to rejoice in you."

"No. No. They'd have to give up unbelief."

"Your God would not be ashamed to see you naked?"

"Wouldn't be my God," she said, "he'd be my beloved."

"Don't say that here. You could get us killed."

"Oh, they have all this stuff in their books," she said. "They just don't believe it."

"Will they ever?" he asked.

"Yes. When they are dying, they grab hold of their women and beg not to go."

"And the women, do they believe?"

"Yes," she said, "When the men do."

60. Lost Faith

For the Thirty-second Sunday in Ordinary Time

God is not God of the dead but of the living; for him all are alive.

LUKE 20:38

There was a priest who lost his faith one day while he was saying Sunday mass. So he stopped where he was and came down from the altar and stood at the head of the aisle and said, "I no longer believe. I must stop here."

There was a silence, then a voice came from the congregation: "No. Do not stop. Finish the mass on our belief."

And other voices began to say the same until a murmur filled the church: "Finish the mass on our belief."

So the priest returned to the altar and read through the rest of the mass for them, and distributed communion to them.

And at the end he came down again to the head of the aisle and said, "This has not been a true mass."

And a voice came from the congregation: "Yes, yes it has." And other voices began to say the same until a murmur filled the church.

"Then you do not need me," the priest said.

"Yes. Yes we do."

"I do not believe any more in words of consecration. I do not believe in these strange clothes I have to wear. I do not believe in lording it over you, in taking your money for these masses. I see you out there with your faces touched by beauty and by pain and by distraction and by calm and by quiet and by worry. Yet all I have are these formulas to read that everything will be all right, and I know everything will not. And there are these old texts I have to twist into the twentieth century to have them make any sense. I don't want to be up here."

There was a silence in the church.

"Where do you want to be?" a voice said from the congregation.

Other voices began to say the same until a murmur filled the church. The priest was silent. Then he said, "I want to be with you. And cannot be. I have lost belief."

"We will find it for you," a voice said, and a murmur filled the church.

"How will you do that? Faith is personal."

"No," a voice said.

"No, no," many voices echoed.

"All right," the priest said, "find it for me and I can stay."

There was a silence.

"It is in your love of anyone," a voice said, and yesses filled the church.

"It's in your telling us the truth," another voice said.

The priest said, "I can do that outside, that does not take faith."

"It does take faith," another voice said, and yesses filled the church.

Then the priest said, "But not faith in green vestments and in words of consecration or in ancient texts that are so hard to understand. Let me tell you about last night. I did a wedding. I had a bridesmaid read from Genesis about God forming male and female from the dust of the ground and breathing in a living soul. And she said to me, 'You sure you want this passage? It's weird!' And that's what started me. Not the passage. I love the dust of the ground. The dust of the ground is not here. It's all covered up. It's covered up with words." There was a silence.

Then a voice said, "We have found your faith for you." And many voices said the same until a murmur filled the church.

"I will bring you my dead!" a voice said.

"I will bring you my new child!" said another.

And another said, "I will bring you my bride!"

"I will bring you my groom!"

"I will bring you my new song!"

The voices filled and shook the church.

The priest said, "How is that my faith?" There was a long silence. Then a voice from the congregation said, "How is it not?" And the silence shook the church.

"But that brings me to you and not to God," the priest said, "Or are you God?"

"No," a voice said, and other voices said the same.

"Then who are you?"

"The dust of the ground."

"And where is God?" But he knew and quickly held up his hand for silence, and no voice spoke. Then the priest looked at his hand held up for silence and said, "I am up to my old tricks, am I not?"

"Yes," a voice said from the congregation, and other voices said the same until the murmur filled the church.

61. Better If We Disappear

For the Thirty-third Sunday in Ordinary Time

> You will again tell good men from bad, the servant of God from the man who does not serve him.
>
> MALACHI 3:20

There was a bishop who could cure. He found it out by accident. A man who came to see him had a fatal disease and wanted the bishop to say his funeral mass when the time came. The bishop said yes, and the man asked for a blessing, which the bishop gave, as he usually did, by putting his hand over people's hearts and praying. He did this instead of waving his hand in the air where his ring would flash. It was the ring of the old bishop who had ordained him. He loved it, but not for blessing people. The sick man's shirt was open so the bishop touched his chest. The man stopped shaking. His whole body straightened. A look of absolute knowledge came over his face.

"What happened?" asked the bishop.

"You know!" said the man, "You know!"

That was the day. The word spread, and people began coming to the high mass. They were broken in every possible way, spiritually, physically, and they knew how the bishop cured. They stood in front of him, their arms at their sides, or sat in their chairs, woman and men, with their breasts bared, in absolute silence, with their request reaching out from their faces. And he would place the palm of his hand on them, and whatever was wrong with them changed in some way, even to the point of cure.

But there was a shock in the church: The women had opened their blouses. And the bishop had touched them. The shock translated into a great complaint. The bishop knew of it and could understand the mentality. He himself was frightened by the cures and by the way they were happening. He was a quiet man and was coming apart under the strain of being an instrument of healing. So when the letter came telling him to stop doing what he was doing, he ran off many copies, which he posted in the church and sent to all the parishes and to the press. He had part of it read over the air. He felt free and went back to his ordinary ways and to the music that he loved—early Renaissance, the secular songs as well as the sacred.

But more people came, crowds standing bare breasted before him, coming up in lines to communion, hoping for more than bread. When the next letter came telling him not to preside any more, he said, "Good! Good!" and ran off many copies and sent them out as before. And went back to his scholar's life of music and texts.

But people came to stand across the street. Even on cold nights there were men, women, and children, their breasts bared, looking up at his window for a time before they left. There was always someone there. When the next letter came telling him to leave the city, he published it as quickly as he could and packed to go. But he was stricken with the palsy of the first man he had cured just as he closed his last valise. He barely made it to a chair and phoned for help.

Word spread that he could not leave and why. People began to come again outside the rectory. There were candles this time, but no one looking for a cure. The bishop realized they were praying for him, not for themselves, and that they had bared their breasts for a penance. There were photographers all over the place, concentrating on the women, but sometimes on a well-known man. The photos were selling for fortunes.

The bishop was devastated in soul as well as in body. "I'm just a simple clunk," he said. "What is all this? It's not God, and it's not the devil. And all these cures come from nowhere I know. All I know is music. My beloved music."

The next letter that came he could not publish. It told him to pray that God remove him from this life as soon as possible. And that he should leave in writing as much a history of his sins as he could bear to record, so no one would be tempted afterwards to make anything of him. So with a shaky hand he burned the letter in the ashtray. He wrote down many things about his life, his prejudices, his hatreds. He put down as his largest fault that he had loved something more than God—his music, the early strings and pipes and drums and reeds, the rhythms, the droning sackbuts.

He crossed his hands on his breast where he sat in the chair and asked God to take him as soon as possible for the good of the church. The palsy in his body began to stop. Strength flowed into his frame from his own hands on his own chest. He pulled those hands away as if from a fire. "If I'm well, I have to go out there." The decision before him was so stark it was almost demonic. He could live for those people. Or he could die for the church. "I will live for those people, but I don't know how."

He crossed his hands on his breast again and was completely cured. Then he went out the front door on that cold night. His shirt was opened to the waist. He walked into the crowd and each one he came to reached out and touched him, palm to chest, as if to ratify the cure.

Then he held his hands up and said, "I am not to use them ever again. Not for myself. Not for you. You will destroy me if you ask. I will destroy you if I answer." No one understood, so he tried again: "Beauty unleashes savagery, don't you understand?" But no one did. So he said, "The strong are the weak. They will call your beauty evil!" There was still a silence all around him in the candlelight and in the glare of cameras. "If I keep my power, they will destroy you," he said. "If you keep your illnesses, they will not." No one understood. So he said the only thing left him. "It is better if we disappear into one another." And they understood.

He turned, went up the steps, closed the rectory door, and came back down. Someone gave him a candle. Someone gave him a scarf. And people began to move away together. Soon the cameras could not spot his figure among the rest. They were just people moving. And there were things happening. But the cameras could not see. So they packed up and went home.

And there were letters afterwards, but general ones, to the world. Which need no reply.

62. A Life for a Life

For the Feast of Christ the King

And to give thanks to the Father who has made you fit to share the heritage of God's people in the realm of light.

COLOSSIANS 1:12

There was a woman who had three sons. All three were in the Mafia. She knew things about them that would put them away for good. Not that they had told her. But she could connect the nights they went out with what the papers later said happened on those nights. She knew if she opened her mouth even to them, *she* would be the one put away for good. Her husband had been killed in prison. Not that he said anything, or even would. But because he could.

There was no value left in life for her. Even the priest was on the payroll. She had seen him on TV after some local killings, defending the place where they all lived as a Christian place. She never confessed to him the growing hatred she felt for her own flesh and blood and for all the masks that hid the face of evil. Whatever she did she would have to do quickly. She would get only one chance. She had to find the one act that would reveal all the people she knew for what they were. It would have to be an act she was caught in. She would have no time to say anything to anyone. And it would have to be in public where people from outside the region could know. The local police were on the payroll.

She knew her sons were keeping kilos of cocaine in their rooms, for a few days at a time, before they took them on to some distribution point. So she began to steal a little at a time. She was clever at opening and closing the little bags. And when she had filled several bags, which she hid in her mattress with her paper money, she began to watch the newspapers for some event that would bring someone important to the area where she lived. Then she saw it. A papal visit was planned the next year, for the canonization of a saint who came from close by. A saint she did not understand. He had worked as a high church official in Rome for many years. But the pope being present was enough.

She began to tell her friends her excitement about his coming. They were all friends who had children in the Mafia. And she went often to the rectory until the priest began to say she was becoming a religious fanatic. The sons recognized in her something that aging women in that culture nearly always do; they try to become holy to save their unholy offspring. Then they drift off into a world of their own. She began to show up at places where her sons worked to leave messages about someone who had died many years ago, asking them to have a mass said. The sons recognized the names as dead Mafia people. They were puzzled, but they did what she asked to the point that the priest thought they were religious fanatics too, but then found out they were humoring their mother.

She knew she had to get to a good spot in the cathedral, some-place close to His Holiness. The priest was no help. He was think-ing of himself and the friends he could make. So she pleaded with her sons to get her close to the pope. They went to the priest and said something to him. So he had her deputed as one of the few from the saint's village who would bring up the offertory gifts, the bread and the wine. There would be a woman and a man, both elderly, and a boy and a girl. And there would be two priests to direct them from either side—the woman's priest would be one of them.

The day the pope was to come the woman took out her best black dress and shoes and a marvelous old shawl her grand-mother had made. The dress was ankle length, like a nun's. In fact she looked like a nun when the shawl was over her head. Inside the dress, in pockets she had made, she put the bags of cocaine, placing them here and there so she would not bulge. She had cut many slits in the pleats of the dress so that she could reach the bags easily. And the bags were folded shut. With one quick motion of her hands, the cocaine would spurt out into the air like water.

The pope arrived and was driven in his armored, glassed-in vehicle through the narrow crowded streets. People almost fell out of their windows trying to see him. He came to the cathedral square and spoke to the packed audience, first about the saint, then about the life of holiness all people are called to lead. After that, he entered the great church to begin the mass of canoniza-tion. Many who could not get in went home quickly from the square to watch the mass on TV. It was a great ceremony, with singing and incense and scriptural reading and solemn declara-tions and the papal presence. When the moment came to bring the offertory gifts, the old man, the old woman, the young boy, and the young girl were ushered by the two priests to the table in the center aisle, where the bread and wine were set.

The old woman picked up the bread on its small golden platter, the old man picked up the wine, the boy and girl picked up flowers, and to the choir's singing they moved down the aisle and up into the sanctuary, into the open space flooded by TV lights just before the altar steps, where the pope waited to receive the gifts. Her hand dropped briefly inside her skirt and she brought out a handkerchief and muffled a sneeze, then dried her eyes. But she had broken open a bag of cocaine underneath her dress, and it poured down between her legs onto the red carpet. Then she returned the handkerchief to her pocket and broke open another bag of cocaine, which left a trail as she mounted the steps to the pope to hand him the holy bread. By now the white trails were visible to the cameras, which zoomed in, but not to anyone in the papal party or church. The woman turned from the pope with her hands folded and started down the steps. By now everyone nearby had noticed. They were puzzled by the trails of cocaine, not knowing what it was. She reached inside her blouse, took out another bag and cast it like holy water to the right of her, then another which she flung like holy water to the left of her as she moved down toward the center aisle. People were frozen with astonishment. She entered the aisle casting clouds of cocaine to the left and right, the cameras following her every step.

The smell of cocaine reached knowing nostrils. And there was a muffled cry," She wants to blow up the pope!" Men tumbled from the pews to lay hold of her. They rushed her down the aisle. In the melee someone put a knife in her, then faded into the crowd at the rear of the church. And the pope descended the steps in his full priestly robes. He stooped down and took some of the white substance on his fingers. He knew what it was. He looked up into the cameras, and his face was filled with pain. The cameras quickly switched back to the crowd, where near panic had set in.

People who knew the woman were making for the door. They knew they had to disappear. She had implicated them all. The police made no effort to stop the panic. They knew. The priest pretended he was caught up in the crowd, pretended to resist, pretended to be carried away against his will. The three sons who saw it on TV were out of the house and gone even before the pope knew it was cocaine.

And there began a series of killings, almost from that minute, people trying to silence potential witnesses. Nearly everyone the woman knew disappeared some way or other. There was little for justice to do. The pope finished the mass in a nearly empty church. At the end, he asked for some old requiem vestments. They were brought out. On camera, he changed from white to black. He asked for an old Latin missal. Then with little ceremony, he said a requiem mass, almost by himself, singing and answering his own voice. He did it standing on the spot where the first bag of cocaine had fallen, white against the red on the carpet. Then he walked down the aisle. He saw where the drops of blood began. He put his hands over his face and left.

The woman was not buried from the church. No one would claim her body. She was interred by order of the court in a pauper's grave.

63. Time Does Not Tell

For the Triumph of the Cross

> But on the way they grew impatient and spoke against God and Moses. "Why have you brought us up from Egypt," they said, "to die in the desert where there is neither food nor water?"
>
> NUMBERS 21:5

There was a priest who wanted to turn the clock back. He suffered terribly from change. So he turned it back to when he was young and had learned what was right. The world outside did not follow suit, and life became more unbearable, to the point where he could not cope at all. "I have to survive," he said. So he went to the clock again and turned it forward, past the present, into the future, by many years. There was nothing there, and no one, just space, like the space he had once seen above the Arctic circle, dark gray to light gray and no line between. "I have to survive," he said, so he came back to the present still gray from the future.

"You're no good to me," he said to the clock.

"You're no good to me either," said the clock.

The priest looked up and saw the receptionist of the parish watching him with some worry.

"You're talking to yourself," she said.

"It's that clock," the priest said, "I told that clock it was no good to me."

"You didn't have to tell it twice," she said. "But it's a half-hour off, so you're right. I'll just turn it back."

"No, please," the priest said, "I tried back, and it was too painful."

"Well, I'll just wind it ahead until it's right."

"No, please, there's nothing ahead, just leave it, let it be out of synch, like me."

"Synch or no synch, there's a couple coming who want to get married. They're scheduled for nine o'clock. Then a couple who want an annulment. They're for ten. There's a woman who wants to kill herself at eleven. And you see the chancellor at twelve-thirty about the roof."

"Enough, please," the priest said, "One thing at a time, the way they do in Alcoholics Anonymous. Is the couple here?"

"No, you've got a half-hour by my clock. You're out of time by yours."

"Shall I tell that couple not to marry?" the priest asked.

"No. Tell them they'll love it."

"And that couple for the annulment, shall I tell them no?"

"No, they'll hate marriage without love."

"And what about the woman suicide, what will I tell her?"

"Tell her to keep talking."

"You know the answers," the priest said.

"You've told me them a thousand times," she answered. "And what do you think I do on your days off? People won't wait."

"Life just goes hurtling on," he said. "It's like watering a lawn with your thumb on the hose, before nozzles came along. The water hits you in the eye and you laugh like a fool and let go. Then the water plops out of the hose and gets your feet all wet."

"It's been a long time since you laughed like a fool," she said.

"I don't remember when."

"I do. It was Holy Saturday night, and the bishop had that big shell he was to bless holy water in, then baptize a baby. I saw you in the sacristy when he poured the water in the shell. There was a leak in the bottom and a little jet of water went all over him. Like that statue in Brussels. You were laughing so hard, you couldn't give out communion."

"The choir was mad at me for that. They thought I punctured the shell just to ruin their music. I wouldn't ruin anyone's music."

"Speaking of music," the woman said, "five minutes and you have to face it. Shall I leave this clock a half-hour ahead? You'll be through quicker."

"No, set it right. And don't be too far yourself. I forget answers."

"It's 'No,' 'No,' and 'Keep talking.' It's 'yes' to the roof and 'no' to pay for it. It's 'yes' to funerals at night and 'no' to the extra charge, and 'no' to the champagne and cake for the wedding mass, and 'yes' to the brass quintet for Saturday night. That will bring you to supper. Supper is stew, and you have to eat it or she'll be mad."

"Enough, please. You're as inexorable as that clock."

"You want me different?"

"Yes, please."

"Okay," she said, "there will be love in your hands in a few minutes. And then there'll be hatred. In your hands. And then there'll be life or death, and which it is will depend on how alive you are. Then you'll have to deal with someone sly who has a collar on, then with one bad mortician who makes funny money, then with some crazy kids who think the Last Supper was a blast, and then with a quintet that will be all the rage in a few years. And you have a chance to live and love like no one else."

The priest was silent. The woman glowed with a kind of ferocity.

"You like me this way?" she asked.

"Yes. Fix the clock and send the couple in. And stay for dinner, please. I can't face that stew alone."

64. Stories to Grow On

For All Souls' Day

Well I know that I shall see the
goodness of the LORD
in the land of the living.

PSALM 27:13

A man was carrying flowers out to his father's grave. It was All
Souls' Day. His car was in the shop, his wife was running errands
in hers, and his three kids were off in their cars to a horse show,
a crayfish hunt, and a ballet tryout. So he was taking a bus to the
cemetery. It was a short walk from the busstop to the grave. On
the bus there was a small boy and his mother between him and
the window, the boy standing against her legs, looking at the
flowers and the man. The boy said, "What are those?"

"Flowers," the man said.

"I mean what for?"

"Shhh!" the mother said. "Leave the man be."

The boy was quiet for a minute then looked from the flowers to
the man's face, not saying a word but with the question still alive
in his eyes.

"They are for my father's grave," said the man.

"My father doesn't have a grave, he went down over the water."

"Oh love," said the mother, "there'll be nothing ever buried in
you." She looked at the man and said, "He's six and got a hero. His
dad was Air Force, and the plane hit another one near it, and they
both went down. War games. So my man is gone. Now this is my
man." She put a hand on the boy's head and he leaned into it. The
man with the flowers was quiet.

Then the boy said, "Could your daddy fly?"

And the man said, "No, but he sure could talk, tell stories day
and night."

"You tell me one?"

"Well, I could, but they're not big stories, like your Daddy could tell, about airplanes and things, just little stories about a country far away where he came from."

"Now leave the man be," the woman said to her boy. She looked at the man and said, "His daddy didn't tell stories, he used to pick him up and fly him all over the house, up stairs, down stairs, I had a lot of broken stuff from these two."

The boy smiled and doubled backwards over his mother's lap and looked up at her with the question still all over his face. The mother combed his eyebrows with her thumb.

"Well," the man said, "he told me once about the banshees." At this the boy straightened up with fascination, tried to say the word and couldn't. "Banshees," the man repeated. "They are beautiful women, and they sit out off the shore on rocks, and they wail when something is going to happen to the fishermen at sea. Anyone walking along the shore who can hear them knows that something bad is going to happen to someone. My father said he heard a banshee wail the day before he went fishing one time and he should have known, but he was young and never minded danger. So he went out in a boat with some other youngsters like himself, but with one old man along who knew where the fish were.

"The old man sensed there was something wrong, so early in the afternoon he begged the boys to sail for home. But they were catching fish after fish and felt they could lick any sea if it rose. And rise it did after a short while, and the boat pitched up and down and sideways in a squall of rain and wind, until my father thought they were done for. The sail was still up and stuck, and the wind was tipping them over. So my father took a hand ax and shinnied up the mast and cut the sail rope at the top even as he swung back and forth, from water on one side to water on the other. They threw all the fish and all their equipment overboard to lighten ship, and they took buckets and bailed and kept it afloat while the storm carried them back in toward the bay where they had come from.

"They were lucky with that squall. They got home safe. But ever after when my father heard the banshee wail, he walked the beach and prayed for the men who were at sea, that they would come home safe."

The man stopped. His eyes were wet. He looked down into the flowers. They were green carnations, foolish hybrid things, but they were the closest to Irish he could find. The boy was pleased with the story and he rubbed against his mother like a small bear.

"He was old when he died?" the woman asked.

"Yes."

"My family has no old men. We're service people. Some last, but not many. We just have women's stories. And they are not enough for him."

"What did he do next?" the boy asked.

"Oh now, love, listen, you never get enough, the man has something sad and he must be quiet."

"It's okay," the man said, "No one asks like this anymore. So I forget how much I loved him."

And this time the woman's eyes were wet. She looked down at the boy. "Isn't that the worst thing," she said, "worse even than the death—to forget how much you love someone?"

"Yes," the man said. "It's so you can go on living, but it's the worst."

"Did he go back out in that boat?" the boy asked.

"Yes, one more time."

"Why only one more time?"

"Something funny happened, and he figured he wasn't for the sea."

"What?" the boy asked.

"Well, he had on this sweater that was too big for him. And he caught a huge salmon on a hand line. You know, just a thin, thin rope with a hook on the end. So he hauled in on the line and managed to pull the fish up over the side of the boat, but as he did, he pulled too hard and fell backward over the seats and the fish fell, too, flapping like crazy and somehow got up inside his loose sweater and began to whack him with head and tail until he was black and blue and another fisherman got the salmon out from under the sweater and onto the bottom of the boat. They were all laughing. But my father figured he wasn't meant for the sea."

And the boy squirmed again against his mother. "And what did he do next?"

The woman looked at the man with some chagrin. She pointed to the cemetery disappearing behind the bus. "You missed it. I'm sorry."

"It isn't far back," he said. "Next, my father took to skipping school. But maybe I shouldn't tell. Give you bad ideas."

"Pretend you won't," the boy said.